The CHELSEA MISCELLANY

By CLIVE BATTY

VSP

Vision Sports Publishing
19–23 High Street
Kingston on Thames
Surrey
KT1 1LL

www.visionsp.co.uk

Published by Vision Sports Publishing in 2012

Text © Clive Batty
Cover illustrations © Steve Gulbis
Inside illustrations © Bob Bond Sporting Caricatures

ISBN 13: 978-1-907637-72-8

Printed and bound in China by
Toppan Printing Co Ltd

Typeset in Sabon MT by Palimpsest Book Production Limited,
Falkirk, Stirlingshire

A CIP catalogue record for this book is
available from the British Library

Author's Acknowledgements

I would like to thank fellow Chelsea fans Mark Colby, Dave Key, Des O'Reilly and Bob Wheeler for providing some useful ideas for this book, and for showing at least mild interest down the pub when I bombarded them with Blues trivia. Alex Leith and Nick Worger, despite both being Brighton supporters, also came up with some worthwhile suggestions. Special thanks are due to Chelsea statistician Derek Webster, a Blues fan for over 50 years, who wrote to me pointing out a number of inaccuracies and omissions in a previous edition of this book and suggesting some new entries for this one.

Bob Bond, whose work has appeared in a variety of Chelsea publications over the years, produced some fantastic cartoons for the book, while thanks are also due to the Editorial Director at Vision Sports Publishing, Jim Drewett, his business partner Toby Trotman and, last but by no means least, my editor, Alex Morton.

Clive Batty

Author's note: All the stats in *The Chelsea Miscellany* are correct up until the start of the 2012/13 season.

Foreword
By Alan Hudson

I'm delighted to write the foreword to this book by my good friend Clive Batty. It's full of facts, records, stats and quirky stories about Chelsea and I'm sure that all Blues fans will find it a really entertaining read.

I was born around the corner from Stamford Bridge and, although I was a Fulham supporter as a boy, Chelsea became my club. I was about 12 when I started training at the Bridge on Tuesday and Thursday nights and it was a fantastic experience because some of the first-team players, like Terry Venables, George Graham and Eddie McCreadie, would always help out. We had little goals set up either side in the big space behind the goal at the Shed End and there would be about 40 of us kids from all over London taking part, going on and off at different times.

I made my debut for the first team aged 17 and became a regular at 18, and what helped me was that the established players, most of whom were five or six years older than me, knew me from those early days. My debut wasn't exactly brilliant – we lost 5–0 at Southampton – so I was much happier when my second game went a lot better, a 1–1 draw at Tottenham. It was just the biggest thrill to be up against the great Jimmy Greaves, but also to be playing alongside the likes of Peter Osgood, Charlie Cooke, Peter Bonetti and Marvin Hinton. To watch Cooke and Osgood as a kid was amazing, and to get in the team and play with them was incredible. They were footballing gods to me.

In my first season we won the FA Cup for the first time in the club's history, which was fantastic, although unfortunately I missed the final against Leeds through injury. The next season we won the European Cup Winners' Cup against Real Madrid in quite weird circumstances, playing two finals in three days. I remember sitting in my hotel room at about 6am in the morning with my medal, looking out over the Athens rooftops and thinking, "is this a dream?" because it all just seemed to happen in a blur. I've got to say, though, that our fans were unbelievable, because a lot of them had only booked a one-night trip and when the final went to a replay they stayed on with virtually no money, sleeping on the beaches. They were magnificent.

Reading through this book brings back a lot of memories of those times. Like the evening when we beat Luxembourg side Jeunesse Hautcharage 13–0 at the Bridge, still Chelsea's record win. I've never felt sorry for another team, but I did that night – I just wish it had been Leeds we were playing! I'm pleased to see that my famous 'goal that never was' against Ipswich also gets a mention. Although it was a decent shot I knew it wasn't a goal, but I felt I deserved it in a way as I'd had two perfectly good goals against Manchester United ruled out earlier that season.

There's quite a bit inside these pages too about 'Blue is the Colour', the song we recorded after reaching the 1972 League Cup Final. We got to number five in the charts and were on Top of the Pops. When we were walking into the studio the Bee Gees were coming out, and it's one of my big regrets that I didn't grab Barry Gibb and get him to record with us!

Browsing through the book, though, there's loads of stuff I didn't know, for instance that Chelsea had a fully qualified doctor playing for them in the 1920s. Or that they once played two games on the same day. And I didn't know, either, that on two occasions they've had to borrow a kit from another team!

Getting back to the present, I was amazed by Chelsea's Champions League success in 2012. I truly believe that some things are written in the stars, and I think it was just meant to be. Having the best goalkeeper in the world in Petr Cech was a big factor in their victory, and I think too that the club made the most fabulous signing they've made for a long time in Gary Cahill. Since they bought him, they've looked a lot tighter at the back. For the real Chelsea supporters, who have followed the club through thick and thin over many years, it was absolutely brilliant to win the Champions League, and I was really happy for them.

As you'd expect, there's lots about that triumph inside these pages – and so much more besides. For any Chelsea fan this is an absolutely fantastic little book, and one I know you'll really enjoy reading.

Alan Hudson

— THEY SAID IT . . . —

"Chelsea is not a normal club because they expect to be the best in the world."
Avram Grant, November 2007

"The Double has never been done before by Chelsea Football Club, and all of us are delighted to go down in the club's history."
Skipper John Terry reflects on the Blues' triumphs in the Premier League and FA Cup, May 2010

"I think some of the English lads at Chelsea run the club, pretty much."
Arsenal goalkeeper Wojciech Szczesny suggests player power is rife at Stamford Bridge, March 2012

"AVB rapidly came to resemble a young captain, trained on the playing fields of Eton, arriving to command a battle-weary platoon at Passchendaele."
Richard Williams in *The Guardian* on the sacking of Andre Villas-Boas, March 2012

"My fiancé Frank [Lampard] cooks quite a lot. He made a massive chilli recently for our guests. Unfortunately the glass lid he put on the saucepan cracked and a million pieces shattered into the chilli, so we ordered a takeaway."
Christine Bleakley reveals that Frank Lampard is unlikely to win *MasterChef* any time soon, January 2012

"You wonder if David Luiz is being controlled by a 10-year-old in the crowd with a Playstation."
Sky pundit Gary Neville is unimpressed by Chelsea's Brazilian defender, November 2011

"It's funny, I only live five minutes from the training ground and we have to be in at 10am, yet I leave home at 8.45 every day. I'm excited and want to come in and train."
John Terry reveals he's unlikely to be fined for arriving late for training, February 2008

"I would love to gather all the fans together to say goodbye but they would crush me with their love."
Jose Mourinho, after leaving Chelsea in September 2007

"Jose Mourinho has denied being over-confident, but he has insisted on Chelsea driving to away games in an open-top bus."
They Think It's All Over **presenter Lee Mack, November 2005**

"Chelsea we know well, a strong team. I like their stadium, Stadium Bridge. I think people realised who I was in England after we played there."

Barcelona superstar Lionel Messi, 2008

"Cheese has been replaced by chalk at Chelsea. The manager with the most theatrical body language in Europe has given way to a manager whose body language is on mute." **Sky commentator Clive**
Tyldesley after Avram Grant replaced Jose
Mourinho, *Daily Telegraph*, November 2007

"Chelsea are being managed by Frank Spencer, the well-intentioned but accident-prone half-wit from *Some Mothers Do 'Ave 'Em*."

***The Sun*'s Steven Howard is unimpressed by**
Claudio Ranieri, December 2001

"Under Mourinho fun was strictly rationed, like sweets in wartime."

David Lacey in his match report for *The Guardian* after Chelsea beat
Manchester City 6–0, October 2007

"John is the ideal stereotypical captain. On and off the pitch, he communicates and gets everyone together. He has that strong personality."

Frank Lampard on John Terry, 2008

"Dennis Wise could start a fight in an empty room."

Alex Ferguson, August 1997

"A man born in Glasgow will die, on average, eight years earlier than a man born in Chelsea." **Good news for local Blues fans,**
***Observer Magazine*, September 2002**

"I like to think that, apart from being a bit of a butcher, I've got something else to offer." **Ron 'Chopper' Harris, 1979**

"I don't want to change what works. I just want to help take what we have at Stamford Bridge to the next level. And I want us all to work hard and have a lot of fun doing it." **Roman Abramovich, August 2003**

"What was incredible was going into the Chelsea dressing room to have a chat and swap shirts. It's bigger than my house."

Norwich midfielder Dickson Etuhu is amazed at
how the other half live, February 2007

"He used to come in every morning and say the same thing, 'Hello, lovely boys, let's have some fun!'"

Scott Minto, on Ruud Gullit's relaxed management style at Chelsea, Talksport, November 2007

"He's a fantastic manager and I'd love to work with him again. I'm sure he'd love it and maybe one day he could be England manager."

John Terry suggests Jose Mourinho is the man to succeed Steve McClaren, November 2007

— UP FOR THE CUP —

Peter Osgood scores in the 1970 FA Cup Final v Leeds

To date, Chelsea have appeared in 11 FA Cup Finals, winning seven and losing four. The Blues first got to the final of the world's oldest knockout football tournament in 1915, when they faced Sheffield United. The match was dubbed the 'Khaki Cup Final' because of the large numbers of uniformed servicemen in the crowd. Sadly for Chelsea fans, the Blues' defence proved easier to penetrate than the German lines in World War One and the Londoners went down to a 3–0 defeat.

After losing to Tottenham in the 'Cockney Cup Final' in 1967, Chelsea returned to Wembley three years later to play arch rivals Leeds. The match finished in a 2–2 draw, the first post-war final to require a replay. The Wembley pitch was deemed too poor to stage the rematch so the replay was moved to Old Trafford. In a bruising, physical encounter, the Blues eventually triumphed 2–1 after extra-time with goals from Peter Osgood and David Webb.

More recently, the Blues beat Middlesbrough 2–0 at Wembley in 1997 to win the cup for a second time. The match is often remembered for Robbie di Matteo's 43-second goal, the quickest in a Wembley final at the time.Chelsea enjoyed a third FA Cup victory in 2000 in the last final to be played under the Twin Towers. Once again, Di Matteo was the hero, scoring the only goal of the game against Aston Villa.

Then, in 2007, Chelsea won the first FA Cup final to be played at the new Wembley. Didier Drogba's winning goal against Manchester United, four minutes from the end of extra-time, secured the Blues their first ever FA Cup and League Cup double. In 2009 the Blues won the FA Cup for a fifth time, goals by Didier Drogba and Frank Lampard seeing off Everton after Louis Saha had given the Toffees a first-minute lead. The following year, Chelsea were back at Wembley to clinch the second leg of 'The Double', Drogba finally breaching Portsmouth's obdurate defence with a well-struck free-kick that proved to be the winner. Then, in 2012 the Blues won the cup for the fourth time in six seasons, beating Liverpool 2–1 in the final at Wembley.

The full list of Chelsea's FA Cup Final appearances is:

Year	Result	Venue
1915	Sheffield United 3 Chelsea 0	Old Trafford
1967	Tottenham 2 Chelsea 1	Wembley
1970	Chelsea 2 Leeds 2	Wembley
1970	Chelsea 2 Leeds 1	Old Trafford
1994	Manchester United 4 Chelsea 0	Wembley
1997	Chelsea 2 Middlesbrough 0	Wembley
2000	Chelsea 1 Aston Villa 0	Wembley
2002	Arsenal 2 Chelsea 0	Millennium Stadium
2007	Chelsea 1 Manchester United 0	Wembley
2009	Chelsea 2 Everton 1	Wembley
2010	Chelsea 1 Portsmouth 0	Wembley
2012	Chelsea 2 Liverpool 1	Wembley

— WHY BLUE IS THE COLOUR —

Chelsea's famous blue shirts stem from the fact that the racing colours of the club's first president, the Earl of Cadogan, were light blue (officially 'Eton blue'). During their inaugural season in the Football League, 1905/06, Chelsea sported pale blue shirts before switching to a darker blue for the first time for the home game against Nottingham Forest on 9 February 1907.

For many years, Chelsea's shorts were white, accompanied either by navy blue or white socks. Royal blue shirts and shorts, set off by white socks, only appeared as a combination together at the start of the 1964/65 season and have since been adopted as the club's 'official' home colours.

— THE BIGGEST TEAM PHOTO . . . EVER! —

The world's biggest ever team photo was taken at Stamford Bridge on 7 August 2006 when 7,000 Blues fans joined manager Jose Mourinho, his squad of players and backroom staff in the traditional pre-season snap. During the 2006/07 season a gigantic version of the original photo could be seen along the outer wall of the stadium, opposite the West Stand.

— DIDIER'S INTERNATIONAL RECORD —

Didier Drogba

Powerful striker Didier Drogba has scored more goals for his country while with Chelsea than any other Blues player. The Ivory Coast player passed Jimmy Greaves' old record of 16 international goals when he found the net in a 1–0 win over Guinea on 7 February 2007. Here's the full list of Chelsea's most prolific international goal scorers:

Player	Country	Goals
Didier Drogba	Ivory Coast	45
Frank Lampard	England	23
Hernan Crespo	Argentina	16
Jimmy Greaves	England	16
Salomon Kalou	Ivory Coast	16
Tore Andre Flo	Norway	15
Eidur Gudjohnsen	Iceland	15
George Hilsdon	England	15
Tommy Lawton	England	15
Andriy Shevchenko	Ukraine	14

— STAMFORD THE LION —

Matchdays at the Bridge wouldn't be the same without Stamford the Lion, Chelsea's long-serving mascot. Here are a few highlights from the colourful life of the club's favourite feline:

1980 Stamford makes his Chelsea debut, cheering up the crowds watching Second Division football at the Bridge. Within weeks he is featured in the opening sequence of 'Match of the Day'.

1983 A great moment as Stamford appears on the cover of the programme for the New Year's Eve clash with Brighton.

1993 Stamford appears in a special edition of 'It's a Knockout!' on the BBC programme 'Standing Room Only'.

1994 The rise of the Chelsea mascot continues as Stamford gets his own column in the matchday programme.

1996 A makeover for Stamford: he loses his tail and has a mane trim.

1998 Stamford is mysteriously kidnapped during a Chelsea-Arsenal match at the Bridge. After a few weeks he turns up in a package addressed to Sky TV football presenter, and Chelsea fan, Tim Lovejoy.

2000 Stamford beats Carlo Cudicini from the penalty spot in the pre-match warm-up before a home game with Tottenham. His goalscoring exploits earn him a double-page spread in the official Chelsea magazine.

2002 In a three-way penalty shoot-out competition at Stamford Bridge against fellow mascots Elvis Junior Eel (Southend United) and Clarence the Dragon (Northampton), Stamford finishes in a disappointing third place.

2005 Stamford's spot-kicking skills let him down again in a London mascot penalty competition won by QPR's Jude the Cat.

2005 Stamford is kidnapped again, shortly before the start of the 2005/06 season. He is returned home a few days later.

2010 Stamford takes part in the London Marathon, completing the 26-mile course in six hours 25 minutes and raising more than £10,000 for Help a London Child in the process.

— DOCTOR AT LARGE —

In the early 1920s Chelsea players had no need to worry about receiving prompt and effective medical treatment if they sustained an injury on the field of play as one of their team-mates was a fully qualified doctor! Signed from Scottish amateur side Queen's Park in 1920, Dr John Bell was a nippy right-winger who continued his medical duties after turning professional with Chelsea. During a three-year stay in west London he played 44 games for the Blues, scoring ten goals.

— JOSE'S SPATS —

During his three years at Chelsea, the colourful and charismatic Jose Mourinho had a number of entertaining run-ins with his fellow managers, the football authorities and the police:

- **With Rafael Benitez:** "We were good friends until Liverpool started winning," Benitez once said, and it's certainly true that Mourinho's relationship with the Liverpool boss deteriorated after the Reds' controversial Champions League victory over Chelsea in April 2005. The following year, the Chelsea manager refused to shake hands with Benitez after both the FA Cup semi-final and the Community Shield and thereafter never missed an opportunity to point out exactly how many points the Merseysiders were behind the Blues in the Premiership.
- **With Sir Alex Ferguson:** During the 2007 title race run-in, Mourinho suggested that under "new football rules" it was "forbidden to give a penalty against Manchester United and forbidden to give any penalties in favour of Chelsea." United boss Ferguson was unimpressed, saying "Mourinho seems to be on some sort of personal crusade. It is a rant all the time. I don't think it's fair to the game."
- **With David Moyes:** The Everton manager was seething when, in December 2006, Mourinho suggested that a penalty box dive by Andy Johnson showed that the Toffees' striker was "untrustworthy". Everton promptly issued a statement backing their player and threatening legal action if Mourinho didn't apologise, which he subsequently did.
- **With Arsene Wenger:** The Arsenal manager threatened Mourinho with legal action in October 2005 after the Chelsea boss described Wenger as "a voyeur" who was obsessed with the Blues. "He likes to watch other people," sneered Mourinho. "He speaks, speaks, speaks about Chelsea." The Blues manager backed up his argument by claiming that he had a 120-page dossier full of Wenger's anti-Chelsea comments, but after the League Managers' Association called for a truce the row blew over.

- **With the Premier League:** In June 2005 Mourinho was fined £200,000 (later reduced to £75,000) for breaching Premier League rules by meeting Arsenal full back Ashley Cole in the Royal Park Hotel, Lancaster Gate, to discuss a possible transfer to Chelsea.
- **With UEFA:** Mourinho's claim that referee Anders Frisk had spoken to Barcelona boss Frank Rijkaard during half-time of the Barca-Chelsea Champions League clash in February 2005 sparked one of European football's most heated controversies. Uefa referee chief's Volker Roth described Mourinho as "an enemy of football", while Uefa accused Chelsea of "making false declarations" and "deliberately creating a poisoned and negative ambience" before hitting the Blues boss with a two-match suspension and a fine of around £9,000.
- **With the police:** In February 2005 Mourinho was escorted by police from the touchline at the Millennium Stadium, Cardiff, after making a 'hush' gesture to Liverpool fans following Chelsea's equaliser in the 2005 Carling Cup Final. Neither the police nor the Football League took any further action, and Mourinho later claimed that his gesture was aimed at a critical media rather than opposition supporters. Then, in May 2007, Mourinho was arrested and cautioned by police in a bizarre dispute over his pet Yorkshire terrier, Leya. The police claimed the dog was in breach of quarantine laws, a charge denied by the Chelsea manager. The somewhat farcical incident was resolved when Leya returned to Portugal with Mourinho's wife, Tami.

— PENALTY SHOOT-OUT AGONY AND ECSTASY —

The full record of Chelsea's involvement in the cup lottery from 12 yards:

Date	Comp	Rd	Match result	Shoot-out outcome
25 Oct 1983	League Cup	2	Chelsea 2 Leicester 2*	Won
13 Nov 1985	Full Members	S/f	WBA 2 Chelsea 2	Won
18 Feb 1991	Full Members	3	Chelsea 1 Luton 1	Lost
26 11 1992	Full Members	3	Chelsea 2 Ipswich 2	Won
8 Feb 1995	FA Cup	4	Chelsea 1 Millwall 1	Lost
17 Jan 1996	FA Cup	3	Newcastle 2 Chelsea 2	Won
3 Aug 1997	Comm Shield		Chelsea 1 Manchester Utd 1	Lost
15 Oct 1997	League Cup	3	Chelsea 1 Blackburn 1	Won
7 Jan 1998	League Cup	5	Ipswich 2 Chelsea 2	Won
26 Oct 2005	League Cup	3	Chelsea 1 Charlton 1	Lost
1 May 2007	Champs Lge	S/f	Liverpool 1 Chelsea 1*	Lost
5 Aug 2007	Comm Shield		Chelsea 1 Manchester Utd 1	Lost

21 May 2008	Champs Lge	Final	Chelsea 1 Manchester Utd 1	Lost
12 Nov 2008	League Cup	4	Chelsea 1 Burnley 1	Lost
9 Aug 2009	Comm Shield		Chelsea 2 Man Utd 2	Won
2 Dec 2009	League Cup	5	Blackburn 3 Chelsea 3	Lost
19 Feb 2011	FA Cup	4	Chelsea 1 Everton 1	Lost
21 Sep 2011	League Cup	3	Chelsea 0 Fulham 0	Won
19 May 2012	Champs Lge	Final	Bayern Munich 1 Chelsea 1	Won

* Aggregate score over two legs

— EUROPEAN ROLL CALL —

The full list of clubs Chelsea have played in European competition:

Austria: Vienna Sport-Club, Austria Memphis
Belgium: Bruges, Anderlecht, Genk
Bulgaria: CSKA Sofia, Levski Sofia
Cyprus: Apoel Nicosia
Czech Republic: Viktoria Zizkov, Sparta Prague
Denmark: BK Frem, FC Copenhagen
England: Manchester City, Arsenal, Liverpool, Manchester United
France: Marseille, Monaco, Paris St Germain, Bordeaux
Germany: Munich 1860, Stuttgart, Hertha Berlin, Bayern Munich, Werder Bremen, Schalke, Bayer Leverkusen
Greece: Aris Salonika, Olympiakos
Holland: DWS Amsterdam, Feyenoord
Israel: Hapoel Tel Aviv
Italy: Roma, AC Milan, Vicenza, Lazio, Juventus, Inter Milan, Napoli
Latvia: Skonto Riga
Luxembourg: Jeunesse Hautcharage
Norway: Tromso, Valerenga, Viking Stavanger, Rosenborg
Portugal: Porto, Benfica
Romania: CFR Cluj
Russia: CSKA Moscow, Spartak Moscow
Scotland: Morton
Slovakia: Slovan Bratislava, MSK Zilina
Spain: Barcelona, Real Madrid, Zaragoza, Betis, Mallorca, Valencia, Atletico Madrid
Sweden: Atvidaberg, Helsingborg
Switzerland: St Gallen
Turkey: Galatasaray, Besiktas, Fenerbahce
Yugoslavia: Red Star Belgrade

Of these clubs, Chelsea have played Barcelona most often (15 meetings since 1966) – although Liverpool (10 meetings since 2005) are catching up fast!

— GOALS GALORE —

In September 1971 Chelsea began their defence of the European Cup Winners' Cup against Luxembourg cup winners Jeunesse Hautcharage. Hailing from a village with a population of just 704, Jeunesse were hardly known in their own country let alone in the wider football world.

Faced by a team of steel workers, a butcher, a blacksmith and a hairdresser, the Blues strolled to a 8–0 victory in the first leg in Luxembourg. Back at the Bridge two weeks later on 29 September 1971, Chelsea recorded their biggest ever win, 13–0, to set a new aggregate 21–0 record for a European tie. The record still stands today, although it was equalled by Feyenoord the following season in the Uefa Cup. Over the two legs Chelsea's 21 goals were scored by Peter Osgood (8), Tommy Baldwin (4), Peter Houseman (3), John Hollins (2), David Webb (2), Ron Harris and Alan Hudson.

In domestic football Chelsea's most emphatic victory was 9–1 against Worksop in the FA Cup in 1908. The Blues' biggest wins in all competitions are listed below:

Competition	Result	Year
European Cup Winners' Cup	Chelsea 13 Jeunesse Hautcharage 0	1971
FA Cup	Chelsea 9 Worksop 1	1908
Football League	Chelsea 9 Glossop 2	1906
League Cup	Doncaster 0 Chelsea 7	1960
Premiership	Chelsea 8 Wigan Athletic 0	2010
Full Members Cup	Chelsea 6 Plymouth 2	1988
Champions League	Galatasaray 0 Chelsea 5	1999
	Chelsea 5 Genk 0	2011
UEFA/Fairs Cup	Chelsea 5 Morton 0	1968
Charity Shield	Chelsea 3 Newcastle 0	1955

— WINNING RUNS —

Chelsea have twice won a club record nine consecutive matches. At the start of the 2005/06 season the Blues beat Arsenal (Community Shield), Wigan, Arsenal, West Brom, Tottenham, Sunderland, Anderlecht (Champions League), Charlton and Aston Villa before Liverpool brought the run to an end, with a 0–0 draw at Anfield in the Champions League.

Then, during the 2007/08 season, Chelsea defeated Newcastle, Fulham, QPR (FA Cup), Everton (Carling Cup), Tottenham, Birmingham, Everton (Carling Cup), Wigan and Reading before being held to a draw at Portsmouth.

— HERE TODAY, GONE TOMORROW —

A team of internationals who all made fewer than 25 appearances each for Chelsea before moving on to pastures new:

1. Alex Stepney (England)
2. Christian Panucci (Italy)
3. Paul Parker (England)
4. Jiri Jarosik (Czech Republic)
5. Khalid Boulahrouz (Holland)
6. Maniche (Portugal)
7. Brian Laudrup (Denmark)
8. Juan Sebastian Veron (Argentina)
9. Clive Allen (England)
10. George Weah (Liberia)
11. Miniero (Brazil)

— BRIDGE BEAUTIES —

Stamford Bridge was the unlikely venue for the West London heat of the Miss Great Britain Beauty Contest of 1977. The event took place in the Chelsea Executive Suite, where a judging panel consisting of midfielder Garry Stanley, manager Eddie McCreadie, June Mears (wife of Chelsea chairman, Brian) and the Mayor and Mayoress of Hammersmith weighed up the girls' assets. The winner was a stunning brunette. "I wasn't surprised because Stanners was a brunette man," a friend of Stanley's later revealed.

— CHAMPIONS IN 1955 —

Chelsea: 1955 First Division Champions

In 1955, in the club's 50th anniversary year, Chelsea won the First Division title for the first time. Led by manager Ted Drake and featuring stars such as skipper Roy Bentley, winger Eric 'The Rabbit' Parsons and future England boss Ron Greenwood, the Blues pipped reigning champions Wolves, Portsmouth, Sunderland and Manchester United to the title in a closely-fought race.

Chelsea secured top spot with a 3–0 win over Sheffield Wednesday on 23 April 1955, and finished the campaign four points ahead of their nearest rivals. After the match, Drake told the supporters: "I have all the honours first-class soccer has to offer – but this tops the lot of 'em. Chelsea are the grandest club I have ever known. I am that pleased that Chelsea have won the title that I don't really know what to say. It has taken us a long time – but then look how long it took Sir Gordon Richards to win the Derby!"

Few Blues fans cared that the club's total of 52 points was the lowest by a championship side in a 42–match league programme. Here's how the table looked at the end of the season:

	P	W	D	L	F	A	Pts
Chelsea	42	20	12	10	81	57	52
Wolves	42	19	10	13	89	70	48
Portsmouth	42	18	12	12	74	62	48
Sunderland	42	15	18	9	64	54	48
Manchester United	42	20	7	15	84	74	47
Aston Villa	42	20	7	15	72	73	47
Manchester City	42	18	10	14	76	69	46
Newcastle United	42	17	9	16	89	77	43
Arsenal	42	17	9	16	69	63	43
Burnley	42	17	9	16	51	48	43
Everton	42	16	10	16	62	68	42
Huddersfield Town	42	14	13	15	63	68	41
Sheffield United	42	17	7	18	70	86	41
Preston North End	42	16	8	18	83	64	40
Charlton Athletic	42	15	10	17	76	75	40
Tottenham Hotspur	42	16	8	18	72	73	40
West Bromwich Albion	42	16	8	18	76	96	40
Bolton Wanderers	42	13	13	16	62	69	39
Blackpool	42	14	10	18	60	64	38
Cardiff City	42	13	11	18	62	76	37
Leicester City	42	12	11	19	74	86	35
Sheffield Wednesday	42	8	10	24	63	100	26

— OSSIE'S CUP RECORD —

Peter Osgood

Chelsea legend Peter Osgood is the last player (and the only Blues player) to have scored in every round of the FA Cup. In 1970 Ossie scored against Birmingham, Burnley, Crystal Palace, QPR (three goals), Watford and Leeds during the Blues' cup run which, of course, ended with skipper Ron Harris lifting the famous old trophy at Old Trafford.

Strangely, up to 1970 it was not that unusual for a player to score in every round of the FA Cup. The last player to do so before Osgood was Jeff Astle for West Bromwich Albion, just two years earlier in 1968.

— HATE FIGURES —

These opposition players' past misdeeds ensured they always received a hot reception from the home fans at the Bridge:

Emlyn Hughes: While playing for Blackpool, the squeaky-voiced defender broke Peter Osgood's leg during a League Cup tie at Bloomfield Road in October 1966. "There was a clash of shins, I wasn't wearing pads, it wasn't compulsory in those days, and I just heard this crack," recalled Ossie. "The pain that followed was terrible."

Gary Sprake: The Leeds goalkeeper kicked Blues midfielder John Boyle in the face during the 1967 FA Cup semi-final between the sides. Boylers suffered a bloody nose and thick lip, but battled on to help Chelsea win 1–0. Sprake later apologised, telling him "John, I promise you, I only meant to kick you in the chest!"

Dean Saunders: Chelsea defender Paul Elliott's career was ended after he sustained a serious knee injury following a tackle with Liverpool striker Saunders at Anfield in September 1992. Elliott later sued Saunders claiming the tackle was reckless, but lost the court case in 1994. Blues fans, though, never forgave the Welshman and gave him a hard time on his subsequent visits to the Bridge.

Stephen Hunt: In the first minute of Chelsea's visit to Reading in October 2006, Hunt's knee clipped Petr Cech's head as the Blues goalkeeper dived on the ball. Cech's skull was broken in the incident and, on his return to action three months later, he was forced to wear a special skull cap for protection. Hunt has since been booed by Chelsea fans whenever the teams meet.

Emmanuel Eboue: A rash challenge by the Arsenal midfielder broke three bones in John Terry's foot at the Emirates Stadium in December 2007, sidelining the Chelsea skipper for two months. Lining up against the Blues in the return fixture in March 2008, Eboue was loudly booed by the home fans.

Wayne Bridge: A popular figure during his six-year stay in SW6, the Manchester City left-back turned the Chelsea fans against him when he refused to shake John Terry's hand before a game at Stamford Bridge in February 2010 following media reports that the Chelsea skipper had had an affair with Bridge's ex-girlfriend, Vanessa Perroncel.

— 'GATLING GUN'S' STUNNING DEBUT —

On 1 September 1906 George Hilsdon made a remarkable debut for Chelsea by scoring five goals at the Bridge in the Blues' 9–2 thrashing of Glossop North End. The former West Ham striker, whose quick-fire shooting earned him the nickname 'Gatling Gun', had written himself into the Chelsea books in his very first game.

Forty-eight years later, on 16 October 1954, amateur player Seamus O'Connell made an equally dramatic entry on to the Chelsea scene, hitting a hat-trick for the Blues at home to mighty Manchester United. Sadly for Seamus he still finished on the losing side as United won an incredible game by the unlikely-sounding score of 6–5.

A number of players have scored two goals on their Chelsea debuts, including:

Year	Player	Result
1905	Francis O'Hara	Chelsea 6 1st Battalion Grenadiers 1 (FA Cup)
1905	Frank Pearson	Lincoln City 1 Chelsea 4
1919	Jack Cock	Chelsea 4 Bradford Park Avenue 0
1920	Buchanan Sharp	Chelsea 2 Blackburn Rovers 1
1947	Bobby Campbell	Chelsea 4 Aston Villa 2
1964	Peter Osgood	Chelsea 2 Workington 0 (League Cup)
1982	David Speedie	Chelsea 2 Oldham Athletic 0
1983	Kerry Dixon	Chelsea 5 Derby County 0

— GRAHAM'S GAFFES —

With a record four own goals to his name 1970s defender Graham Wilkins is the Blues' very own answer to the hapless Mr Bean. The teams to benefit from Wilko's generosity were Bolton (1976), Manchester City (1977), Aston Villa (1979) and West Ham (1980). Graham, though, could lose his unwanted record some time in the future as current Chelsea captain John Terry has already notched three own goals (against Arsenal in the FA Cup and Bolton in the Premiership, both in 2003, and against Barcelona in the Champions League in 2006) and is likely to play for the club for some years to come. Michael Essien, too, will be crossing his fingers that he doesn't add to the own goals he scored against Reading (2006), Tottenham (2007) and Liverpool (2012).

On five occasions, the own goal bug has been catching with a pair of Chelsea players netting at the wrong end:

- On 5 October 1963, both Bobby Tambling and Ron Harris scored for Stoke in a 3–3 draw at Stamford Bridge.

- 11 years later 'Chopper' was on the scoresheet for Stoke again, this time with Mickey Droy, as the Blues crashed 6–2 in the League Cup at the Victoria Ground on 22 October 1974.
- On 27 March 1976 David Hay and, yes, you've guessed it, Graham Wilkins found the target for Bolton in their 2–1 victory over the Blues at Burnden Park.
- On 5 February 1983 Chelsea goalkeeper Steve Francis and midfielder John Bumstead both scored at the wrong end in the Blues' 3–1 home defeat by Derby.
- Erland Johnsen and Craig Burley both experienced that sinking feeling after netting for Coventry in a 2–2 draw at Highfield Road on 4 February 1995.

— DOUBLE BOOKED! —

On 18 November 1905 the Blues played two first-team games on the same day, at home to Burnley in the league and away to Crystal Palace in the FA Cup.

The double-header resulted from the FA's insistence that Chelsea would not be given exemption from the preliminary rounds of the FA Cup, unlike other Second Division sides, because of the Blues' late election to the league a few months earlier. The first two rounds of the competition didn't clash with league games, and Chelsea were able to field strong teams on both occasions. In the third round, however, the match with Palace fell on the same day as Burnley's trip south. Ordered by the Football League to put out their strongest team against the Lancastrians, Chelsea's FA Cup run came to a premature end as their reserves, including two new players who had been registered at the last possible moment, were thrashed 7–1 by the Eagles. At least there was some consolation back at the Bridge, where Chelsea beat Burnley 1–0.

This somewhat farcical episode caused a rethink at FA headquarters, where a resolution was passed insisting that clubs must field full-strength teams in all matches in the FA Cup.

— 2010: A YEAR TO REMEMBER —

No Chelsea fan will ever forget the 2009/10 season as the Blues, under then manager Carlo Ancelotti, swept to the club's first-ever league and cup 'Double' and so joined an elite group of six other clubs – Preston North End, Aston Villa, Tottenham Hotspur, Arsenal, Liverpool and Manchester United – who had previously claimed the two major domestic prizes in English football in the same season. What's more, Chelsea won the 'Double' in some style, setting a number of significant records along the way:

- The Blues' total of 103 league goals set a new high for the Premier League, no club previously having recorded three figures in the 'goals for' column.
- Chelsea's goal difference of +71 was an all-time best for the top flight of English football.
- The Blues became the first club in Premier League history to score seven or more goals in four league games, defeating Sunderland 7–2, Aston Villa 7–1, Stoke City 7–0 and Wigan Athletic 8–0.
- Ashley Cole and Nicolas Anelka became the first-ever players to win the 'Double' with two different clubs, both having previously achieved the same feat with Arsenal – Anelka in 1998 and Cole in 2002.
- Following the Blues' 1–0 defeat of Portsmouth in the FA Cup Final at Wembley, Ashley Cole became the first-ever player to win the cup six times. His previous triumphs were with Arsenal in 2002, 2003 and 2005, and with Chelsea in 2007 and 2009.
- In winning the FA Cup, Chelsea only conceded one goal in the tournament – in a 4–1 victory over Cardiff City in the fifth round – equalling the post-war best for defensive meanness.
- Chelsea coach Carlo Ancelotti became the first Italian manager to win the league title and only the second Italian boss to win the FA Cup – after Chelsea's Gianluca Vialli in 2000.

John Terry: Double-winning captain

— THE WIT AND WISDOM OF KEN BATES —

Chelsea chairman from 1982 to 2004, Ken Bates was never afraid to speak his mind. Here are some of his most memorable utterances . . .

"The Romans did not build an empire by organising meetings. They did it by killing anyone who got in their way."
**Plaque on the wall in the main reception at Stamford Bridge.
It has now been removed**

"It wasn't a football club, it was a social club with a bit of football played on Saturdays, occasionally." **On taking over as chairman**

"If shutting Chelsea solved the hooligan problem I would do it tomorrow, but it wouldn't." **After a pitch invasion by fans in 1985**

"Poverty among fans is grossly exaggerated when you see what they spend elsewhere. A small minority are poor and can't afford it."
Dismissing suggestions that Chelsea's ticket prices are too high

"Our fans were systematically abused all evening without any provocation and yet we were fined. A bit like being in a Nazi concentration camp and being charged an admission fee." **On Chelsea's visit to Marseille in 2000**

"Even Jesus Christ only had one Pontius Pilate – I had a whole team of them."**After being ousted from the board of the Wembley Stadium project**

"Experience shows that after a disaster it is particularly difficult with the Americans, who appear to be quite cowardly despite their Rambo films."
Explaining the fall in American visitors to Chelsea Village after 9/11

"Makelele? Who does he play for? I've only heard of his brother, Ukelele."
Thoughts on a potential Chelsea transfer target

"I think it's very interesting that when I took over at Leeds I got loads of messages, telephone calls, emails and letters from Chelsea fans saying, 'Good luck Ken, I'm sure you'll do well there. Make sure you get them up and then we can stuff the bastards.'"
On the intense Chelsea-Leeds rivalry, 2005

"If I had my time again I'd be a general or a bishop."
Reflecting on an alternative career path, 2005

— SWEET SIXTEEN —

Six 16-year-olds have played for Chelsea:

- **Ian 'Chico' Hamilton (16 years 138 days):** Chelsea's youngest ever player scored on his debut at Tottenham in a 1–1 draw in March 1967 but only made four more appearances before being sold to Southend eight months later.
- **Kingsley Whiffen (16 years 157 days):** Welsh goalkeeper who made his only first-team appearance in a 3–2 defeat at Leicester in May 1967.
- **Tommy Langley (16 years 274 days):** Striker who graduated from the Shed terraces to make his debut in a 0–0 draw with Leicester in November 1974. Went on to play 152 games for the club, scoring 43 goals, before being sold to QPR in £425,000 in the summer of 1980.
- **Michael Woods (16 years 275 days):** Ginger-haired midfielder who made his debut as a late substitute for Ashley Cole in the 6–1 FA Cup third round thrashing of Macclesfield in January 2007.
- **John Sparrow (16 years 283 days):** Attacking left-back who was first selected by Blues boss Dave Sexton for the 3–0 home defeat of Burnley in March 1974. Injuries marred his Chelsea career, though, and after making just 74 appearances in seven years he was sold to Exeter in 1981.
- **Mike Harrison (16 years 360 days):** The first 16-year-old to play for Chelsea, Harrison was a left-winger who made his debut against Blackpool in April 1957. Remained at the club for five years as understudy to Frank Blunstone, scoring nine goals in 64 games, before joining Blackburn in 1962.

— CHAMPIONS OF EUROPE! —

After years of agonising near misses, including defeat on penalties against Manchester United in the 2008 final in Moscow, Chelsea finally won the Champions League four years later following a dramatic penalty shoot-out victory against Bayern Munich.

The match, played at Bayern's Allianz Arena home ground, saw Chelsea forced onto the back foot for long periods and the Blues survived a number of scares before they fell behind to a Thomas Muller header in the 83rd minute. However, showing a fighting spirit which had marked their whole European campaign, Roberto di Matteo's men rallied to equalise five minutes later thanks to a magnificent header by Didier Drogba from Juan Mata's corner.

Early in extra time, the Blues conceded a penalty when Drogba fouled Bayern winger Franck Ribery in the box, but Petr Cech kept the Londoners' hopes alive with a superb save from Arjen Robben's spot-kick. With the additional half hour producing no further goals, the final would be decided by penalties. Here's how the shoot-out panned out:

	Bayern	**Chelsea**
Pen 1	Philipp Lahm – scored (1–0)	Juan Mata – saved (1–0)
Pen 2	Mario Gomez – scored (2–0)	David Luiz – scored (2–1)
Pen 3	Manuel Neuer – scored (3–1)	Frank Lampard – scored (3–2)
Pen 4	Ivica Olic – saved (3–2)	Ashley Cole – scored (3–3)
Pen 5	Bastian Schweinsteiger – saved (3–3)	Didier Drogba – scored (3–4)

Drogba's winning kick, calmly slotted into the corner of the goal while Neuer dived the wrong way, meant that Chelsea had won the Champions League for the first time in their history and become the first London club to claim the trophy. As if that wasn't good enough, the Blues also ensured their qualification for the 2012/13 Champions League as holders and, as a consequence, relegated arch rivals Tottenham into the far less prestigious Europa League. Now, that's what you call a triple whammy!

— LONG-RUNNING CUP EPIC —

In 1956, years before the introduction of penalty shoot-outs, Chelsea were involved in one of the longest-running FA Cup ties in history. After 1–1 draws with Burnley at Turf Moor and the Bridge, two further matches at St. Andrews (2–2) and Highbury (0–0) failed to produce a winner. The fourth round saga finally came to an end after 540 minutes, when the Blues defeated the Clarets 2–0 at White Hart Lane. Strangely, Chelsea visited Turf Moor in the league just a few weeks later and the result wasn't close at all – Burnley won 5–0!

— WHAT A WASTE OF MONEY! —

In July 2007 *The Times* produced a list of the 50 worst buys by Premiership clubs since the league's inception in 1992. The club with the poorest record in the transfer list was Newcastle, nine of whose purchases appeared on the list. The article, though, can't have made for comfortable reading in the Stamford Bridge boardroom either as no fewer than eight Chelsea players, bought at a staggering total cost of £89 million, made the cut:

No	Player	Bought from	Date	Fee
49	Khalid Boulahrouz	Hamburg	Aug 2006	£7m
32	Paul Furlong	Watford	May 1994	£2.3m
26	Andriy Shevchenko	AC Milan	May 2006	£30.8m
24	Glen Johnson	West Ham	July 2003	£6m
22	Adrian Mutu	Parma	Aug 2003	£15.8m
13	Chris Sutton	Blackburn Rovers	July 1999	£10m
11	Juan Sebastian Veron	Manchester United	Aug 2003	£15m
9	Robert Fleck	Norwich City	Aug 1992	£2.1m

When, in the same month, *The Times* published a list of the top 50 football transfers just four Chelsea players were featured: 44) Kerry Dixon (£175,000 from Reading in 1983), 26) Michael Essien (£24m from Lyons in 2005), 14) Gianfranco Zola (£4.5m from Parma in 1996) and 10) Petr Cech (£7m from Rennes in 2004). The list was headed by Eric Cantona, who moved from Leeds to Manchester United for a bargain £1m in 1992.

— RED GIFTS —

Chelsea fans aren't complaining, but for some weird reason Manchester United players have had an odd habit of donating own goals to the Blues. To date, six United players have kindly hit the back of the net for Chelsea – and Henning Berg, bless him, has somehow managed the same trick twice:

Year	Own Goal by	Result
1966	Pat Crerand	Man United 1 Chelsea 1
1987	Gary Walsh	Man United 3 Chelsea 1
1990	Gary Pallister	Man United 2 Chelsea 3
1992	Mal Donaghy	Man United 1 Chelsea 1
1997	Henning Berg	Man United 2 Chelsea 2
1999	Henning Berg	Chelsea 5 Man United 0
2012	Jonny Evans	Chelsea 3 Man United 3

— ONE MINUTE OF FAME —

On 22 April 1997, 18-year-old striker Joe Sheerin made his Chelsea debut as a substitute for Gianfranco Zola in the 90th minute of the Blues' 1–0 win against Wimbledon at Selhurst Park. It was a big moment for the rookie forward, but he didn't get a touch of the ball before the final whistle blew and never appeared in the first team again. Still, at least Sheerin, who in a quirk of fate went on to play for AFC Wimbledon, could console himself with the thought that he holds the record for the shortest ever Chelsea playing career.

The ten Blues players to have played just one game for the club as substitute are:

Player	Year	Against	Player Replaced
Roger Wosahlo	1967	Stoke City (H)	Jim Thomson
Jimmy Clare	1980	Bolton Wanderers (A)	Clive Walker
Gerry Peyton	1992	Sheffield Wednesday (H)	Dmitri Kharine
Steve	1993	Manchester	Neil Shipperley

Livingstone		United (A)	
Joe Sheerin	1997	Wimbledon (A)	Gianfranco Zola
Steve	1997	Blackburn (H)	Mark Hughes
Hampshire		Lge Cup	
Leon Knight	2001	Levski Sofia (A)	Gianfranco Zola
		UEFA Cup	
Anthony Grant	2005	Manchester United (A)	Joe Cole
Jimmy Smith	2006	Newcastle United (A)	Ricardo Carvalho
Jacob Mellis	2010	MSK Zilina (H) CL	Josh McEachran

— SUPER-FIT COE GETS BLUES RUNNING —

Shortly after becoming Chelsea manager in 1979 Geoff Hurst brought in Olympic athlete and keen Blues fan Seb Coe to train the team once a week. "He gave new meaning to the term 'being fit'," recalled left winger Clive Walker. "We would do ten runs of 60 yards each and he would do double that amount with ease. On one occasion we were up against each other in a 60-yard race and we were both dipping for the line, it was that close. He simply impressed us by being a super-fit guy – he was on a level which we'd never achieved. It really helped us having him around, he was top drawer."

Coe's training sessions seemed to be paying dividends as the Blues surged to the top of the Second Division table and looked all set for promotion. However, following a late season dip in form, they ended up missing out on a return to the top flight on goal difference. Coe himself did rather better, winning a gold medal in the 1,500m and a silver in the 800m at the 1980 Moscow Olympics.

— BLUE TWEETS —

The most popular Chelsea-related Twitter sites include:

Chelsea FC	@chelseafc	1,005,588 followers
Juan Mata	@juanmata10	869,739 followers
David Luiz	@DavidLuiz_4	185,823 followers
John Terry	@JohnTerryGMF	117,314 followers
Fernando Torres	@FTorresGMF	94,294 followers
Raul Meireles	@RaulMeireles 4	46,582 followers
Drogba Foundation	@FoundationDrogba	22,420 followers

— CHELSEA IN THE WHITE HOUSE —

In 1992, when Bill Clinton became American President, Blues fans were intrigued to learn that the Clintons had a daughter called Chelsea. Some supporters immediately assumed that this was a clear sign that the new incumbent at the White House was a fellow Blue. After all, hadn't Bill lived in Oxford, only an hour's drive from the Bridge, during his student days (when, famously, he had smoked pot but hadn't 'inhaled')?

However, Clinton soon revealed the real reason why he and his wife, Hilary, had named their daughter 'Chelsea' – and it had nothing to do with the football club. Instead, Bill and Hil had chosen the name after their favourite song, *Chelsea Morning* by Canadian singer Joni Mitchell (although, wisely, they decided to drop the 'Morning' bit). Nevertheless, Ms Clinton joins a short list of famous people who are lucky enough to be able to say, 'Chelsea is my name':

Name	Profession
Bobby Frederick Chelsea Moore	England football captain
Viscount Chelsea	Aristocrat
Chelsea Field	Actress
Chelsea Beauchamp	Singer
Chelsea Noble	Actress
Chelsy Davy	On/off girlfriend of Prince Harry
Chelsea Cooley	Miss USA 2005
Chelsea Handler	US comedienne
Chelsea Kane	Actress
Chelsea Korka	Singer
Chelsea Norris	DJ
Chelsea Peretti	US comedienne
Chelsea Wolfe	Singer

— WEDDING BELLS —

Following the Marriage Act of 1994 a number of football grounds, including Stamford Bridge, were granted licences to conduct marriages under the new legislation from 1 April 1995. Among the first couples to get hitched at the Bridge were:

18 August 1995	Andrea and Alun Chappell
21 February 1996	Kate and 'Binny' Binfield
3 August 1996	Dawn and Peter Fairminer
9 November 1996	Donna and Danny Young

— CHAMPIONS 'DOUBLED' —

On just two occasions Chelsea have recorded 'doubles' over the season's eventual champions. In 1958/59 the Blues beat Wolves 6–2 at the Bridge and 2–1 at Molinuex. Despite these results, the Midlands club went on to win the league by six points while Chelsea had to settle for 14th place.

More recently, in the 1993/94 season, Chelsea beat 'Double' winners Manchester United home and away. Gavin Peacock was the Blues' hero in both games, scoring the only goal in 1–0 wins at the Bridge and Old Trafford.

— BULLDOG BRITS AND JOHNNY FOREIGNERS —

On Boxing Day 1999 Chelsea sparked a press storm by becoming the first English club to field a team entirely consisting of overseas players. The Blues side which won 2–1 at Southampton was made up of two Frenchmen (Frank Leboeuf and Didier Deschamps), two Italians (Roberto di Matteo and Gabriele Ambrosetti), a Romanian (Dan Petrescu), a Nigerian (Celesetine Babayaro), a Dutchman (Ed de Goey), a Norwegian (Tore Andre Flo), a Uruguayan (Gus Poyet), a Brazilian (Emerson Thome) and a Spaniard (Albert Ferrer).

The last time Chelsea fielded a team wholly made up of British players was against Leicester City at Filbert Street on 6 May 1995. Even so, one of the players, Mark Stein, had been born in South Africa. The other ten British-born Blues were Kevin Hitchcock, Steve Clarke, Scott Minto, Frank Sinclair, David Lee, Nigel Spackman, Craig Burley, Gavin Peacock, David Hopkin and Paul Furlong.

— CHELSEA'S SHORTEST SEASON —

When, in September 1939, Adolf Hitler decided to invade Poland he not only brought an end to the 'Peace in our time' promised by British Prime Minister Neville Chamberlain, but also called a premature halt to the 1939/40 football season.

Like other teams in the First Division, the Blues had played just three games when the Football League season was suspended the day after Britain's formal declaration of war against Germany on 3 September. For those of you who are too young to remember or were too busy practicing air-raid drills to care, here are Chelsea's results in full from the truncated season:

Date	Result
27 August 1939	Chelsea 3 Bolton Wanderers 2
31 August 1939	Chelsea 1 Manchester United 1
2 September 1939	Liverpool 1 Chelsea 0

— PLAYER OF THE YEAR —

The Chelsea Player of the Year award was established in 1967, in memory of long-serving chairman Joe Mears who had died the previous year. Ray Wilkins holds the record as the youngest player to win the award, being just 19 when he first topped the poll in 1976. The oldest winner is the evergreen Gianfranco Zola, who was 37 when he claimed the trophy for a second time in 2003. The full list of winners is as follows:

Year	Player
1967	Peter Bonetti
1968	Charlie Cooke
1969	David Webb
1970	John Hollins
1971	John Hollins
1972	David Webb
1973	Peter Osgood
1974	Gary Locke
1975	Charlie Cooke
1976	Ray Wilkins
1977	Ray Wilkins
1978	Mickey Droy
1979	Tommy Langley
1980	Clive Walker
1981	Petar Borota
1982	Mike Fillery
1983	Joey Jones
1984	Pat Nevin
1985	David Speedie
1986	Eddie Niedzwiecki
1987	Pat Nevin
1988	Tony Dorigo
1989	Graham Roberts
1990	Ken Monkou
1991	Andy Townsend
1992	Paul Elliott
1993	Frank Sinclair
1994	Steve Clarke
1995	Erland Johnsen
1996	Ruud Gullit
1997	Mark Hughes
1998	Dennis Wise
1999	Gianfranco Zola
2000	Dennis Wise

2001	John Terry
2002	Carlo Cudicini
2003	Gianfranco Zola
2004	Frank Lampard
2005	Frank Lampard
2006	John Terry
2007	Michael Essien
2008	Joe Cole
2009	Frank Lampard
2010	Didier Drogba
2011	Petr Cech
2012	Juan Mata

— THE OTHER STAMFORD BRIDGE —

Confusingly for some, there is a village called Stamford Bridge in Yorkshire which is famous for being the site of the battle in September 1066 in which Harold II of England defeated an invasion by his brother Tostig and Harald III of Norway. A month later Harold had less luck when he came up against another invading force led by Duke William (later William I) at the Battle of Hastings.

Incidentally, Stamford Bridge derives its name from the bridge that spans the railway line alongside the ground, rather than from the battle site.

— 'A BOBBLE HAT AND A BUTCH WILKINS SCARF, PLEASE' —

Sample items from the Chelsea Club Shop, 1977:

Bobble hat	95p
'Butch Wilkins' scarf	85p
Chelsea dart flights	50p
Rosette	25p
Chelsea jeans belt	85p
Chelsea mug	60p
Chelsea action pen	70p
Chelsea car sticker	20p
Team shirt (large)	£4.50
Chelsea medallion	£10

— THE £196 MILLION TEAM —

Chelsea fielded their most expensively assembled team ever in a Premier League game away to Blackpool on 7 March 2011. Boasted by the recent additions of David Luiz and Fernando Torres, the Blues' starting line-up at Bloomfield Road cost an eye-watering £196.4 million in transfer fees, despite including one homegrown player in skipper John Terry:

Player	Fee
Petr Cech	£7 million (from Rennes in 2004)
Jose Bosingwa	£16.2 million (from Porto in 2008)
John Terry	N/A
David Luiz	£21 million (from Benfica in 2011)
Ashley Cole	£5 million (from Arsenal in 2006)*
Michael Essien	£24.4 million (from Lyon in 2005)
Ramires	£19.8 million (from Benfica in 2010)
Frank Lampard	£11 million (from West Ham in 2001)
Yuri Zhirkov	£18 million (from CSKA Moscow in 2008)
Fernando Torres	£50 million (from Liverpool in 2011)
Didier Drogba	£24 million (from Marseille in 2004)

* Plus exchange deal with William Gallas moving to Arsenal

— FA CUP FINALS AT THE BRIDGE —

In the years immediately before the construction of Wembley Stadium, Stamford Bridge was the venue for three FA Cup Finals (results below). The ground has also hosted ten FA Cup semi-finals, the most recent in 1978 when Arsenal beat Orient 3–0.

Year	FA Cup Final result	Attendance
1920	Aston Villa 1 Huddersfield Town 0	50,018
1921	Tottenham 1 Wolves 0	72,805
1922	Huddersfield Town 1 Preston 0	53,00

— SUCCESSFUL SKIPPERS —

John Terry is the most successful captain in the history of Chelsea. To date, the England defender has lifted 10 major trophies for the Blues: the Premier League in 2005, 2006 and 2010; the FA Cup in 2007, 2009, 2010 and 2012; the Carling Cup in 2005 and 2007 (although on the latter occasion, Terry had left the pitch injured and Frank Lampard raised the trophy); and, best of all, the Champions League in 2012 (sharing cup-collecting duties with Lampard as Terry missed the game through suspension).

The full list of trophy-winning Chelsea captains is as follows:

Captain	Number of Major Trophies Won
John Terry	10
Dennis Wise	4
Ron Harris	2
Roy Bentley	1
Terry Venables	1

— BLACK EASTERS —

In 1959 Chelsea journeyed up to Blackpool at Easter and were hammered 5–0. The following day Ted Drake's team travelled across the Pennines to Leeds and did slightly better, only succumbing 4–0.

Unbelievably, the Blues fared even worse over the same holiday period 27 years later. On Easter Saturday 1986 John Hollins' men were crushed 4–0 at home to West Ham and, two days later, went down to another humiliating defeat, 6–0, on the plastic pitch at Queens Park Rangers. To add to the Blues' woes, striker David Speedie was sent off at Loftus Road.

— ALIEN INVASION? —

In quite possibly the most bizarre incident in the history of Chelsea FC, four UFOs were spotted hovering over Stamford Bridge on 10 March 1999 during the FA Cup sixth-round replay between the Blues and Manchester United. The sighting of the alien aircraft was made by an on-duty policeman – rather than, as you might have imagined, a fan who had downed one too many pre-match pints in the Butcher's Hook pub – who reported four diamond-shaped lights moving "across the sky fairly quickly, changing shape slowly." The X-files-style episode eventually became public knowledge in 2010, when the Ministry of Defence released 6,000 pages of material relating to UFO sightings in Britain.

Unsurprisingly, there are still many unanswered questions. Were the aliens long-distance Chelsea supporters, who decided to travel across the universe to London from their own planet after picking up grainy satellite images of Dennis Wise & Co. in action? Why haven't they returned to the Bridge to see another game? At the very least, you would have thought, they could have popped back to do the stadium tour and, afterwards, buy a few souvenirs in the Megastore. But no, nothing. Given that the Blues lost that 1999 match 2–0, should we assume that the inter-galactic visitors are that most depressing of species – fair-weather fans?

— CHEERS REF! —

The decisions that had Chelsea fans thanking the match officials:

- In the final minute of the 1967 FA Cup semi-final Chelsea were leading Leeds 1–0 at Villa Park when the Yorkshiremen were awarded a free-kick just outside the Blues' area. The ball was knocked sideways to United midfielder Peter Lorimer who struck a powerful shot past Chelsea goalkeeper Peter Bonetti and into the top corner. However, Leeds' celebrations were cut short when referee Ken Burns disallowed the goal, on the grounds that he had not blown his whistle for the free-kick to be taken.

- On 26 September 1970 Chelsea beat Ipswich Town 2–1 at Stamford Bridge, but one of their goals sparked a major controversy when *Match of the Day* cameras clearly showed that Alan Hudson's 20-yard shot had rebounded from the stanchion outside, rather than inside, the goal. Ipswich manager Bobby Robson was incensed, and vainly pleaded for the match to be replayed. Hudson later admitted that he knew the ball had not gone in, but had decided not to inform the referee, Roy Capey.

- In the final minute of the FA Cup fifth round replay between Chelsea and Leicester at Stamford Bridge on 26 February 1997 the score was still deadlocked at 0–0. In a last-ditch attack, Blues centre-back Erland Johnson surged into the Leicester box where he appeared to lose control of the ball before colliding with Foxes defenders Spencer Prior and Matt Elliott. To the dismay of the Leicester players, referee Mike Reed pointed to the spot. Frank Leboeuf took full advantage of the dubious penalty award, slotting his shot into the corner of the goal to secure Chelsea a place in the last eight.

- In the Champions League last 16 tie with Barcelona at Stamford Bridge on 8 March 2005 Chelsea were leading 3–2 on the night but trailing on the away goals rule when they were awarded a corner deep into the second half. Damien Duff took it, and John Terry met the cross to head past Barca keeper Victor Valdes for the winning goal. Barcelona's complaints that Valdes had been impeded by Ricardo Carvalho were ignored by Italian referee Pierluigi Collina.

- With the Blues trailing Tottenham 1–0 at Stamford Bridge on 30 April 2011, Frank Lampard fired a speculative 30-yarder that squirmed under the dive of Heurelho Gomes before the Spurs goalkeeper quickly turned to grab the ball right on the line. However, assistant official Mike Cairns indicated that Lampard's shot had crossed the line and a goal was awarded. The Blues enjoyed another stroke of luck late in the game when Salomon Kalou's winner was allowed to stand, despite appearing to have been struck from an offside position.

— MOST SURPRISING TRANSFER —

Imagine one of Chelsea's top players, John Terry or Juan Mata for example, leaving the Blues to join a lower division side for a record transfer fee. It just wouldn't happen. Yet, in November 1947, that's precisely the scenario which unfolded when Chelsea's England international Tommy Lawton left the Bridge for Notts County, then in the Third Division (South). The fee, £20,000, was a record for Britain at the time. Despite his drop down the divisions, Lawton continued to be picked for England and finished his international career with the remarkable record of 22 goals in 23 games.

— PLAY-OFF ONE-OFF —

Chelsea are the only side in the modern era to have been relegated from the top flight in a play-off. So-called 'Test' matches were originally used to decide promotion and relegation issues in the 1890s, and were re-introduced as 'play-offs' in 1986/87. The following season Chelsea finished in the play-off position (18th) in the old First Division and had to fight for their survival with three Second Division clubs, Middlesbrough, Blackburn and Bradford City. After beating Blackburn in the semi-final (6–1 on aggregate), the Blues faced Middlesbrough in the final. Following a 2–0 defeat in the first leg at Ayresome Park, Chelsea could only manage a 1–0 win at the Bridge in the return and were relegated. Serious crowd trouble after the match led to the FA ordering the closure of Chelsea's terracing for the first six games of the next season and also resulted in the play-off system being modified to only include clubs attempting to gain promotion.

— DOUBLE CHAMPIONS —

By winning the Premiership two years in succession in 2005 and 2006 Chelsea joined an elite group of clubs to have retained the league title. The other clubs to have achieved this feat are: Preston (1889, 1890), Sunderland (1892, 1893), Aston Villa (1896, 1897 and 1899, 1900), Sheffield Wednesday (1903, 1904 and 1929, 1930), Liverpool (1922, 1923; 1976, 1977; 1979, 1980; and 1982, 1983, 1984), Huddersfield (1924, 1925, 1926), Arsenal (1933, 1934, 1935), Portsmouth (1949, 1950), Manchester United (1956, 1957; 1993, 1994; 1996, 1997; 1999, 2000, 2001; 2007, 2008 and 2009) and Wolves (1958, 1959).

— NAUGHTY BOYS —

During the 2000/01 season the Chelsea matchday programme asked the Blues' squad what was the naughtiest thing they did as a child. Here is a selection of their answers:

Sam Dalla Bona: "I slashed my sofa when I was five or six with a knife. I can't remember why I was so angry. My parents just slapped me and bought another."

Jesper Gronkjaer: "We found some frozen strawberries in the freezer, and started throwing them at a neighbours' door. They had a white wall. Then it became red!"

Eidur Gudjohnsen: "When I was ten or eleven and living in Reykjavik me and a couple of mates broke into our school and sprayed fire extinguishers."

Kevin Hitchcock: "When I used to live in Plaistow as a kid, we used to go to the top of the maisonettes and launch eggs at bus drivers and people getting off buses."

Jes Hogh: "In a cooking class at school my friend threw a wet cloth at me. I caught it and threw it back at him, but he ducked and it hit the teacher in the face. She went mad and threw me out of the class for the rest of the year."

Graeme Le Saux: "I left a fish head in a girl's pencil case once in biology. We were dissecting fish and she wouldn't do it as she didn't like fish.

She opened her pencil case in the next lesson, home economics, and found the fish head."

John Terry: "We had a mad geezer on our estate. When he came out, a few of the lads were hiding and egged him and threw flour at him so it stuck. He used to chase us, but he never caught any of us."

Gianfranco Zola: "While my father was loading his lorry, I found a knife and completely cut the seat where I was sitting. The lorry was new and my father was not best pleased."

— DEBUT BOYS —

The greatest number of Chelsea players to make their first-team debut in the same match is 11 for the Second Division game against Stockport County at Edgeley Park on 2 September 1905. The fact that this was the Blues' first ever match helped, of course.

Otherwise, the record stands at nine. Bill Robertson, Danny Winter, Albert Tennant, Robert Russell, John Harris, Reg Williams, Tommy Lawton, Len Goulden and Jimmy Bain all made their Chelsea debuts in the third round (first leg) FA Cup tie at home to Leicester City on 5 January 1946. Again, though, this was a statistical oddity explained by the six-year gap in first-class fixtures during World War II.

In more normal circumstances, the record number of players to make their Chelsea debuts in the same match is six, set on 13 August 2003 against MSK Zilina in the Champions League qualifying round (Wayne Bridge, Glen Johnsen, Geremi, Juan Sebastian Veron, Damien Duff and Joe Cole) and equalled on 15 August 2004 against Manchester United at Stamford Bridge (Petr Cech, Paulo Ferreira, Alexey Smertin, Didier Drogba, Ricardo Carvalho and Mateja Kezman).

— SIGNED FROM ITALY XI —

In recent years Chelsea have made a habit of buying players from Italy's Serie A. Here's a whole team recruited from the land of pasta, ice cream and gondolas:

1. Carlo Cudicini (from Castel di Sangro, 1999)
2. Luca Percassi (from Atalanta, 1998)
3. Mario Stanic (from Parma, 2000)
4. Marcel Desailly (from AC Milan, 1998)
5. Ruud Gullit (from Sampdoria, 1995)
6. Roberto di Matteo (from Lazio, 1996)
7. Andriy Shevchenko (from AC Milan, 2006)
8. Didier Deschamps (from Juventus, 1999)

9. Pierluigi Casiraghi (from Lazio, 1998)
10. Gianfranco Zola (from Parma, 1996)
11. Gabriele Ambrosetti (from Vicenza, 1999)
Manager: Gianluca Vialli (from Juventus, 1996)

— SING-A-LONG WITH CHELSEA —

The word 'Chelsea' has appeared in quite a few song titles over the years, largely because it's a famous area in both London and New York. Here, in order of artistic merit, is our Top Five . . . enjoy, pop-pickers:

Song title	Artist	Year Released
1. Chelsea Morning	Joni Mitchell	1967
2. (I Don't Want to Go to) Chelsea	Elvis Costello	1978
3. Chelsea Dagger	The Fratellis	2006
4. Chelsea Monday	Marillion	1983
5. Chelsea Girl	Simple Minds	1979

— STATESIDE BLUES —

In the 1970s football in America experienced a boom, thanks largely to a number of world-class players, including Pele, Franz Beckenbauer and Johan Cruyff, joining NASL teams towards the end of their illustrious careers. Quite a few former Chelsea players hopped across the Atlantic to join them, including this complete team of ex-Blues:

1.	Peter Bonetti	St Louis Stars
2.	John Boyle	Tampa Bay Rowdies
3.	John Dempsey	Philadelphia Furies
4.	Garry Stanley	Lauderdale Strikers/ Wichita Wings
5.	Alan Hudson	Seattle Sounders
6.	Charlie Cooke	Los Angeles Aztecs/ California Surf
7.	Keith Weller	New England Tea Men/ Fort Lauderdale Strikers
8.	Tommy Baldwin	Seattle Sounders
9.	Peter Osgood	Philadelphia Furies
10.	Alan Birchenall	San Jose Earthquakes/ Memphis Rogues
11.	Clive Walker	Fort Lauderdale Strikers
Manager: Eddie McCreadie		Memphis Rogues

— SHARE AND SHARE ALIKE —

The fewest number of Chelsea players to find the net in a single season is seven in 1938/39. Unsurprisingly, given their shot shy attack, the Blues struggled all through the campaign and only avoided relegation to the old Second Division by a single point. At the end of the season Chelsea fans were indebted to leading scorers Joe Payne (17), George Mills (12) and Dickie Spence (11), without whose goals the drop would have been a formality.

At the other end of the scale, the Blues have on four occasions shared their seasonal haul of goals among no fewer than 18 players: in 1909/10, 1996/97, 2003/04 and 2007/08. Normally, a high number of goalscorers would suggest the club had enjoyed a pretty good season, but that was far from the case in 1909/10. Jimmy Windridge was the most prolific of the Blues' 18 marksmen with a paltry six goals and the lack of a regular scorer proved to be a fatal problem for Chelsea, who were relegated after finishing 19th in the First Division.

— LIKE FATHER, LIKE SON —

Most Blues fans know that Frank Lampard's dad played for West Ham but the midfielder is not alone among Chelsea players in following in his father's footsteps. Just check out this complete team of past and present Blues, all of whose dads were also pretty good with the ball at their feet:

Player	Father	Father's (main) club
1. Carlo Cudicini	Fabio	AC Milan
2. John Sillett	Charles	Southampton
3. Neil Clement	Dave	QPR
4. Juan Sebastian Veron	Juan snr	Estudiantes
5. Gavin Peacock	Keith	Charlton
6. Ray Wilkins	George	Brentford
7. Frank Lampard	Frank snr	West Ham
8. Eidur Gudjohnsen	Arnor	Anderlecht
9. Kerry Dixon	Mike	Luton
10. Brian Laudrup	Finn	Brondby
11. Juan Mata	Juan snr	Real Oviedo
Manager: Jose Mourinho	Felix	Vitoria Setubal

— THEIR BOSS IS A BLUE —

The following clubs have been managed in the Premier League by a former Chelsea player:

Arsenal: George Graham (1992–95), Stewart Houston (1996)*
Blackburn Rovers: Mark Hughes (2004–08)
Bradford City: Chris Hutchings (2000)
Chelsea: David Webb (1993), Glenn Hoddle (1993–96)+, Ruud Gullit (1996–98)+, Gianluca Vialli (1998–2000)+, Graham Rix/Ray Wilkins (2000)*, Ray Wilkins (2009)*, Roberto Di Matteo (2012–)
Crystal Palace: Ray Lewington (1998)*
Fulham: Ray Lewington (2007)*, Mark Hughes (2010–11)
Leeds United: George Graham (1996–98), Terry Venables (2002–03)
Manchester City: Mark Hughes (2008–09)
Middlesbrough: Terry Venables (2000–01)<
Newcastle United: Ruud Gullit (1998–99), Steve Clarke (1999)*
QPR: Ray Wilkins (1994–96)+, Mark Hughes (2012–)
Southampton: Glenn Hoddle (2000–01)
Tottenham Hotspur: George Graham (1998–2001), Glenn Hoddle (2001–03), Clive Allen (2007)*
West Brom: Roberto di Matteo (2010–11)
West Ham: Gianfranco Zola (2008–10)
Wigan Athletic: Chris Hutchings (2007)

* Caretaker manager
+ Player/manager
< Joint manager (with Bryan Robson)

— WARTIME GUESTS —

A number of famous names played for Chelsea as guests during the world wars when the Football Association relaxed its normally stringent registration rules. Well-known loan stars appearing at the Bridge included:

World War I: Charles Buchan (the man behind 'Charles Buchan's soccer monthly')
World War II: Walter Winterbottom (future England manager)
Matt Busby (future Manchester United manager)
Joe Mercer (future England manager)
Eddie Hapgood (Arsenal and England)

— HEADS! . . . OR, ER, MAYBE TAILS —

Chelsea's European fate has twice been decided by the toss of a coin. In 1966 the Blues met AC Milan in the third round of the Fairs Cup, the precursor of the UEFA Cup. Milan won the first leg 2–1 before Chelsea triumphed in the second leg at the Bridge by the same score. A play-off match, held in Milan, ended 1–1 after extra-time forcing the tie to be settled by a toss of the coin. Chelsea skipper Ron Harris called correctly and the Blues went through to the next round.

Two years later, in 1968, Chelsea were paired with DWS Amsterdam in the Fairs Cup second round. After two 0–0 draws, the Blues' hopes again relied on Ron Harris' ability to call 'heads' or 'tails' correctly. Sadly, 'Chopper' called incorrectly and the Blues went out.

— JIMMY'S GOAL-FILLED SEASON —

Legendary goal poacher Jimmy Greaves hit a post-war top-flight record 41 league goals in the 1960/61 season, including six hat-tricks. The teams to feel the full force of Greavsie's striking powers were Wolves (three goals in a 3–3 draw), Blackburn (three goals in a 5–2 win), Manchester City (three goals in a 6–3 win), West Brom (five goals in a 7–1 win), Newcastle (four goals in a 6–1 win) and, in his last match for the Blues, Nottingham Forest (four goals in a 4–3 win).

— YOUNG GUN, OLD STAGER —

The youngest player to have appeared for Chelsea is Ian 'Chico' Hamilton, who made his Blues debut at the age of 16 years, 4 months and 18 days against Tottenham at White Hart Lane on 18 March 1967. He headed Chelsea's equaliser in a 1–1 draw.

The oldest player to have pulled on a Blues shirt is Dickie Spence, who was aged 39 years, 1 month and 26 days when he made his final appearance for the club in a 1–1 draw against Bolton Wanderers at the Bridge on 13 September 1947.

Graham Rix became Chelsea's oldest debutant when he came on as a substitute at home to Viktoria Zizkov in the European Cup Winners Cup on 15 September 1994 at the age of 36 years, 10 months and 23 days. Rix, who was Chelsea's youth team coach at the time, was called into service because Uefa's 'foreigners rule' restricted clubs to selecting just three non-English players.

— BLUES BLEMISH FOR GOONERS —

As every footy fans knows, Arsenal won the league in 2003/04 without losing a match. The Gunners' championship side of 1990/91 very nearly matched that feat, losing just one game in the 38-match league programme. The team to wipe the smile from the north Londoners' faces, if only temporarily, was Chelsea who beat Arsenal 2–1 at the Bridge on 2 February 1991. Kerry Dixon and rookie striker Graham Stuart scored for the Blues, with Alan Smith hitting a late consolation goal for the champions-elect.

— ONE-GOAL WONDERS —

As the saying goes, it only takes a second to score a goal. Sometimes, though, it can take a good deal longer – just look at this list of Chelsea players, all of whom played over 100 games for the club, but who only found the net once for the Blues:

Player	Appearances	Goal	Year
George Barber	294	v Brighton (A)	1933
Erland Johnsen	182	v Southampton (H)	1994
Graham Wilkins	149	v Middlesbrough (H)	1979
Albert Ferrer	113	v Hertha Berlin (H)	1999
John Sillett	102	v Doncaster Rovers (A)	1960
Andrew Ormiston	102	v Leicester Fosse (H)	1912

— BLUES BROTHERS —

Four sets of brothers have played for Chelsea. In chronological order, they are William and Christopher Ferguson (1928); Peter and John Sillett (1957–61); Allan and Ron Harris (1963–67); and Graham and Ray Wilkins (1973–79).

Meanwhile, a number of Chelsea players have had brothers who played professionally for other clubs. These include:

Player	Brother
Celestine Babayaro	Emmanuel (Besiktas)
Ian Britton	Billy (Forfar)
Steve Clarke	Paul (Kilmarnock)
Didier Drogba	Joel (St. Pauli)
Tore Andre Flo	Jostein (Sheffield United)
Glenn Hoddle	Carl (Barnet)
John Hollins	Dave (Newcastle)
Salomon Kalou	Bonaventure (Auxerre)
Ray Lewington	Chris (Wimbledon)

Derek Smethurst	Peter (Blackpool)
Alexey Smertin	Yevgeny (Dynamo Moscow)
Mark Stein	Brian (Luton)
John Terry	Paul (Yeovil Town)
Roy Wegerle	Steve (Feyenoord)
Shaun Wright-Phillips	Bradley (Manchester City)

— GRIM CHRISTMAS —

There was little festive cheer for Chelsea fans in 1960 as they saw their team lose 2–1 at home to Manchester United on Christmas Eve. At the time it was customary to play the same team twice in a Yuletide double-header, so on Boxing Day the Blues travelled to Old Trafford where they were on the wrong end of a 6–0 thrashing. The mince pies and Christmas pud tasted no better after the next match, a 6–1 hammering at Wolves on New Year's Eve. Oh well, surely the New Year would bring better luck? Wrong! In their first match of 1961 the Blues crashed out of the FA Cup, losing 2–1 at home to Fourth Division Crewe Alexandra.

— WORLD CUP BLUES —

Chelsea supplied more players to countries competing in the 2006 World Cup than any other club on the planet: 17, two more than nearest rivals Arsenal.

The Blues' previous best tally was 11 players at the 1998 tournament in France. Of this group, Frank Leboeuf and Marcel Desailly went on to become the first Chelsea players to win the World Cup, while Tore Andre Flo, Dan Petrescu and Brian Laudrup all scored, making them the first Chelsea players to get on the scoresheet in the finals.

The full list of World Cup Blues is:

Year	Venue	Players
1950	Brazil	Roy Bentley (England)
1958	Sweden	Peter Brabrook (England)
1966	England	Peter Bonetti (England, unused)
1970	Mexico	Peter Bonetti (England), Peter Osgood (England)
1986	Mexico	Kerry Dixon (England)
1990	Italy	Tony Dorigo (England), Dave Beasant (England, unused)
1994	USA	Erland Johnsen (Norway), Dmitri Kharine (Russia)

1998	France	Celestine Babayaro (Nigeria), Marcel Desailly (France), Albert Ferrer (Spain), Tore Andre Flo (Norway), Ed de Goey (Holland, unused), Brian Laudrup (Denmark), Frank Leboeuf (France), Roberto di Matteo (Italy), Dan Petrescu (Romania), Graeme Le Saux (England), Frank Sinclair (Jamaica)
2002	Japan/Korea	Celestine Babayaro (Nigeria), Marcel Desailly (France), Jesper Gronkjaer (Denmark), Emmanuel Petit (France), Mario Stanic (Croatia)
2006	Germany	Michael Ballack (Germany), Wayne Bridge (England, unused), Ricardo Carvalho (Portugal), Petr Cech (Czech Republic), Joe Cole (England), Hernan Crespo (Argentina), Didier Drogba (Ivory Coast), Michael Essien (Ghana), Paulo Ferreira (Portugal), William Gallas (France), Asier del Horno (Spain)*, Robert Huth (Germany), Frank Lampard (England), Claude Makelele (France), Arjen Robben (Holland), Andriy Shevchenko (Ukraine), John Terry (England)
2010	South Africa	Nicolas Anelka (France), Ricardo Carvalho (Portugal), Ashley Cole (England), Joe Cole (England), Deco (Portugal), Didier Drogba (Ivory Coast), Paulo Ferreira (Portugal), Branislav Ivanovic (Serbia), Salomon Kalou (Ivory Coast), Frank Lampard (England), Florent Malouda (France), John Terry (England)

* Named in the original squad, but withdrew through injury

— LIGHTS OUT! —

One of the strangest episodes in Chelsea history occurred on 29 January 1969 when the Blues were playing Preston in an FA Cup fourth round replay at the Bridge. Two goals to the good, Chelsea appeared to be cruising into the next round when, suddenly, the Bridge floodlights failed with 15 minutes still to play. Referee Ken Burns had no option but to call the game off and the match was re-played the following Monday afternoon, Chelsea winning 2–1 thanks to late goals by David Webb and Charlie Cooke. Despite the game being played on a working day the attendance at the Bridge, 36,522, was only 1,000 down on Chelsea's average for the season – presumably thousands of fans phoned in sick or suddenly remembered they had a funeral to go to . . .

— KEEPING UP APPEARANCES —

Ron Harris lifts the 1970 FA Cup

Chelsea's all-time leading appearance maker is Ron Harris, who played in an amazing total of 795 games following his debut in February 1962. Nicknamed 'Chopper' because of his no-nonsense approach to defending, Ron was the Blues' skipper when Chelsea won the FA Cup in 1970 and the European Cup Winners' Cup the following year. After seeing off his nearest challenger, team-mate Peter Bonetti, Ron left the Blues to become player/coach at Brentford in the summer of 1980.

The top ten Chelsea appearance makers are:

Player	Years Played	Appearances
1. Ron Harris	1962–80	795
2. Peter Bonetti	1960–79	729
3. John Hollins	1963–84	592
4. Frank Lampard	2001–	558
5. John Terry	1998–	547
6. Dennis Wise	1990–2001	445
7. Steve Clarke	1987–98	421
8. Kerry Dixon	1983–92	420
9. Eddie McCreadie	1962–73	410
10. John Bumstead	1978–91	402

— PREMIER LEAGUE MILESTONES —

Date	Milestone	Result
15 Aug 1992	1st goal (Mick Harford)	Chelsea 1 Oldham 1
15 Aug 1992	1st point	Chelsea 1 Oldham 1
29 Aug 1992	1st win	Chelsea 1 QPR 0
23 April 1994	100th point	Chelsea 1 Leeds 1
7 May 1994	100th goal (Mark Stein)	Chelsea 3 Sheffield United 2
6 Feb 1999	100th win	Chelsea 1 Southampton 0
26 Dec 2000	500th point	Ipswich 2 Chelsea 2
8 May 2001	500th goal (Jimmy Floyd Hasselbaink)	Liverpool 2 Chelsea 2
31 March 2007	1,000th point	Watford 0 Chelsea 1
1 Nov 2008	1,000th goal (Alex)	Chelsea 5 Sunderland 0

— TOP GOAL GRABBERS —

Chelsea's all-time highest scorer is 1960s star Bobby Tambling. A Chelsea youth product, Bobby scored for the Blues on his debut in a 3–2 win over West Ham at Stamford Bridge in February 1959 . . . and found the net another 201 times over the next decade. His best haul was five goals away to Aston Villa in September 1966.

1980s hotshot Kerry Dixon threatened to overtake Bobby's longstanding record, but a poor last season at the Bridge when he only scored six goals ruined his chances.

Chelsea's all-time highest scorers are:

Player	Goals	Games	Goals/ Games ratio
Bobby Tambling	202	370	0.55
Kerry Dixon	193	420	0.46
Frank Lampard	186	558	0.33
Didier Drogba	157	341	0.46
Roy Bentley	150	367	0.41
Peter Osgood	150	380	0.39
Jimmy Greaves	132	169	0.78

— BLUE IS THE COLOUR —

To mark their achievement in reaching the League Cup Final in 1972, the glamorous Chelsea team of the period recorded 'Blue is the Colour' at a studio in Islington, north London. Released on Penny Farthing Records the single reached number five in the charts, making it one of the most successful club songs in pop history.

This is how the chart looked in the week Chelsea played Stoke in the League Cup final at Wembley in early March 1972:

1. Nilsson, Without You
2. Don MacLean, American Pie
3. Chicory Tip, Son of my Father
4. New Seekers, Beg, Steal or Borrow
5. Paul Simon, Mother and Child Reunion
6. Michael Jackson, Got To Be There
7. Chelsea FC, *Blue is the Colour*
8. Gilbert O'Sullivan, Alone Again (Naturally)
9. Lindisfarne, Meet Me on the Corner
10. Slade, Look Wot You Dun

— ALL WE ARE SAYING IS GIVE US A GOAL! —

The Blues' worst run in front of goal came towards the end of the 1980/81 season, when the team went nine games without finding the net. The dismal run began on 14 March 1981 with a 1–0 defeat at Bristol Rovers and continued until the opening day of the following season when Colin Lee hit the first goal in a 2–0 defeat of Bolton Wanderers at the Bridge on 29 August 1981. In all, 876 minutes had elapsed since the previous Chelsea goal on 7 March 1981 – ironically, also scored against Bolton, this time by Alan Mayes. The nine games in which the Blues failed to score were:

Date	Result
14 March	Bristol Rovers 1 Chelsea 0
21 March	Chelsea 0 Blackburn Rovers 0
28 March	Newcastle 1 Chelsea 0
4 April	Chelsea 0 Cardiff City 1
11 April	Oldham 0 Chelsea 0
18 April	Chelsea 0 Bristol City 0
20 April	Chelsea 0 Luton Town 2
25 April	Swansea City 3 Chelsea 0
2 May	Chelsea 0 Notts County 2

— BLUE TUNES —

During the 2001/02 season the Chelsea matchday programme asked the players which song the team should run out to. Here are their responses:

Carlton Cole: *Blue Day* (Suggs)
Sam Dalla Bona: *Blue Day* (Suggs)
Marcel Desailly: *Jump* (Van Halen)
Mikael Forssell: *Keep Their Heads Ringin'* (Dr Dre)
William Gallas: *Blue Day* (Suggs)
Ed de Goey: *Blue Day* (Suggs)
Jesper Gronkjaer: *Jump* (Van Halen)
Eidur Gudjohnsen: *Simply The Best* (Tina Turner) or *Eye Of The Tiger* (Survivor)
Slavisa Jokanovic: *We Are The Champions* (Queen)
Jimmy Floyd Hasselbaink: *Tubthumping* (Chumbawamba)
Joe Keenan: *Eye Of The Tiger* (Survivor)
Jody Morris: Theme from *Benny Hill*
Emmanuel Petit: *Blue Day* (Suggs)
John Terry: *Papa's Got A Brand New Pigbag* (Pigbag)
Boudewijn Zenden: *Simply The Best* (Tina Turner)
Gianfranco Zola: *Blue Is The Colour* (Chelsea FC)

— SUPERSTARS CHALLENGE —

In April 1993 some members of the Chelsea squad competed against their fellow professionals in an event organised by *Shoot!* magazine. Dubbed 'Superstars Challenge', the tournament saw the Blues try their luck in four events – shooting, 100m sprint, throw-in and goalkeeper's throw. Here's how they got on:

Event	Top Chelsea player	Time/ distance	Winning time/ distance
Hardest shot	David Lee	80 mph	85 mph
100m	Michael Duberry	11.9 secs	11.7 secs
Throw-in	David Hopkin	37 metres	46.5 metres
Keeper's throw	Dave Beasant	51 metres	56.8 metres

— WEATHER WOES —

- Four Chelsea matches have been abandoned as a result of bad weather. The most recent was on 20 December 1972 when thick fog descended on Carrow Road in the final minutes of the Blues' League Cup semi-final against Norwich, leading ref Gordon Hill no option but to call the game off. With Chelsea trailing 3–2 (and 5–2 on aggregate) this was definitely a lucky break for the Londoners, but it turned out to be merely a stay of execution as the Canaries won the rearranged fixture 1–0 to reach the final.

- On 29 October 1932 the Blues' First Division match against Blackpool at Bloomfield Road went ahead despite a freezing cold wind and sub-zero temperatures – according to the local evening paper: "the worst day climatically for many seasons." In the second half four Chelsea players decided they'd had enough and, living up to their 'southern softies' reputation, rushed off to the warmth of the dressing room. The sturdy northerners remained at full strength and won the match 4–0. Remarkably, Chelsea manager David Calderhead kept the same team for the next match, while the club programme also leapt to the defence of the players who walked off: "Those ready to disparage the quitters should know that in each case the player had barely enough strength left to reach the dressing room before collapsing. Common humanity suggested the game should have been abandoned."

- In recent years the worst conditions Chelsea have played in were in Tromso, northern Norway, in October 1997. With heavy snow falling throughout the second half the pitch markings completely disappeared yet, to Blues boss Ruud Gullit's annoyance, the referee insisted that the match should continue. Tromso won the game, a second round European Cup Winners' Cup fixture, 3–2 but were hammered 7–1 in the return leg at the Bridge when the conditions were much more to Chelsea's liking.

— JIMMY'S THREE-GOAL FIRST —

The first Chelsea hat-trick was notched by Jimmy Windridge in a 5–1 victory over Hull City at Stamford Bridge on 11 September 1905. Windridge, who had joined the Blues from Small Heath (later to become Birmingham City) finished the season with an impressive total of 16 goals in just 20 games, but was pipped to be the club's first ever leading scorer by Frank Pearson, who scored 18 goals in 29 games.

— 'FATTY' FOULKE: CHELSEA'S FIRST SUPER-SIZED SUPERSTAR —

William 'Fatty' Foulke

Willie 'Fatty' Foulke, Chelsea's first goalkeeper and captain, was a huge (in every sense of the word) attraction in the early years of the club. A giant of a keeper signed from Sheffield United, Foulke was 6ft 2 inches tall, weighed a massive 22 stone and wore size 12 boots.

His personality was equally out-sized. Opposition strikers who tangled with him risked being grabbed by the collar and thrown into the net, while it wasn't unknown for Foulke to storm off the pitch in a huff if he felt his team-mates weren't performing adequately. His style as a goalkeeper was surprisingly agile, however, as the very first Chelsea programme pointed out to the fans: "In spite of his bulk he possesses all the activity of a cat, combined with the playfulness of a kitten."

In an effort to intimidate the opposition, Chelsea arranged for two small boys to stand behind Foulke's goal to exaggerate his bulk still further. The plan worked as Foulke kept an amazing nine consecutive clean sheets in his one season stay at the Bridge – a club record which stood for 99 years until surpassed by Petr Cech in the 2004/05 season. The boys also proved useful for collecting and returning the ball when it went out of play behind the goal and so, quite accidentally, the role of 'ball boy' was created.

— WORST RESULT EVER —

Chelsea's heaviest ever defeat was an 8–1 thrashing away to Wolves on 26 September 1953. Remarkably, just over 18 months after this black day in the history of the club, an almost unchanged Blues team had been crowned league champions.

Below is a list of Chelsea's worst defeats in a variety of domestic and European competitions. The squeamish may wish to quickly turn over the page:

Year	Competition	Result
1953	Football League	Wolves 8 Chelsea 1
1905	FA Cup	Crystal Palace 7 Chelsea 1
1974	League Cup	Stoke 6 Chelsea 2
1966	UEFA/Fairs Cup	Barcelona 5 Chelsea 0
2000	Champions League	Barcelona 5 Chelsea 1
1988	Full Members Cup	Swindon Town 4 Chelsea 0
1995	European Cup Winners Cup	Zaragoza 3 Chelsea 0

— KEY DATES IN THE FORMATION OF CHELSEA FC —

28 April 1877: 6,000 people attend the opening of Stamford Bridge, the new home of the London Athletic Club.

29 September 1904: The Mears brothers, Gus and Joseph, take possession of the freehold of Stamford Bridge.

14 March 1905: Fulham FC having turned down the chance to play at Stamford Bridge, the Mears brothers and their colleague Fred Parker decide to form a new club which will apply for league membership.

24 March 1905: The name of the club, Chelsea FC, is chosen in preference to the three other options: Kensington FC, London FC and Stamford Bridge FC.

27 March 1905: John Tait Robertson, a Scottish international half-back, is appointed as player/manager of the new club on a salary of £4 per week.

20 April 1905: Chelsea announce that they are applying for election to the Football League, having received little encouragement from other London clubs for their application to the Southern League.

26–27 April 1905: Chelsea sign their first players: centre-half Bob McRoberts and inside-forwards Jimmy Robertson and Jimmy Windridge. All three arrive from Small Heath (later to become Birmingham City) and the combined fee is just £340. Within the next three weeks another ten players are signed, including 22-stone goal-keeper Willie 'Fatty' Foulke.

29 May 1905: Football League meeting at Tavistock Hotel, Covent Garden. Without having kicked a single ball, Chelsea are elected to the Second Division of the league, along with Leeds City, Hull City and Clapton Orient.

1 September 1905: The Chelsea team travel on the 6.05pm train from Euston to Manchester, ahead of their first ever match at Stockport County. The party stays at the Albion Hotel in Manchester.

2 September 1905: Chelsea's first match in the Second Division ends in a 1–0 defeat.

— THE BEST . . . AND THE WORST —

In June 2007 *The Times* published a list of the world's top 50 footballers. Selected by journalist Gabriele Marcotti, the list was headed by AC Milan star Kaka and also included nine current or former Chelsea players: Hernan Crespo (43), Florent Malouda (31), John Terry (30), Michael Ballack (26), Andriy Shevchenko (26), Didier Drogba (22), Frank Lampard (16), Petr Cech (14) and Michael Essien (5). Apart from Kaka, the other players ranked higher than Essien were Samuel Eto'o, Cristiano Ronaldo and Ronaldinho.

The following month *The Times* went to the other extreme, producing a list of the 50 worst footballers to play in the English top flight since 1970. Five Chelsea players made it into this hall of shame: Jody Morris (47), Winston Bogarde (29), Frank Sinclair (26), Mickey Droy (14) and Vinnie Jones (10). The list was headed by Southampton's Ali Dia, a notorious chancer who falsely claimed to be George Weah's cousin and a Senegalese international. He made just one fleeting appearance for the Saints before his utter uselessness was revealed to all.

— LEAP YEAR FIXTURES —

Chelsea have played just four matches on 29 February:

Year	Competition	Result
1908	FL Division One	Chelsea 2 Sunderland 1
1964	FL Division One	Sheffield Wednesday 3 Chelsea 2
1992	FL Division One	Chelsea 0 Sheffield Wednesday 3
2000	Champions League	Olympique Marseille 1 Chelsea 0

— OUR SHEETS ARE CLEAN . . . —

Chelsea goalkeeper Petr Cech set an English top flight record in 2004/05 by clocking up 1,024 Premiership minutes without conceding a goal. This incredible run fell just 39 minutes of the all-time English record, set by Reading keeper Steve Death in 1979. Cech's ten consecutive shut-outs during this period – against Norwich (4–0), Aston Villa (1–0), Portsmouth (2–0), Liverpool (1–0), Middlesbrough (2–0), Tottenham (2–0), Portsmouth (3–0), Blackburn (1–0), Manchester City (0–0) and Everton (1–0) – broke the longstanding club record of nine clean sheets set by Willie 'Fatty' Foulke in season 1905/06 and, more importantly, helped Chelsea consolidate their position at the top of the Premier League.

Petr Cech: simply the best goalkeeper in the world

— ... AND NOT SO CLEAN —

In season 1960/61 the Blues managed just one clean sheet in 42 league games, a young Peter Bonetti denying the Preston strikers in a 2–0 Chelsea win at Deepdale. The Blues ended the campaign having conceded a club record 100 goals; there was better news at the other end, however, where Jimmy Greaves and co. scored 98 goals – also a club record at the time.

— STADIUMS FROM HELL —

In the 1992/93 season the Chelsea matchday programme asked the players to name their least favourite away ground. Here are their replies:

Dave Beasant: Ayresome Park, Middlesbrough
Tony Cascarino: Springfield Park, Wigan Athletic
Robert Fleck: Plough Lane, Wimbledon
Gareth Hall: The Manor Ground, Oxford United
Kevin Hitchcock: Feethams, Darlington
Erland Johnsen: Selhurst Park, Crystal Palace
David Lee: The Dell, Southampton
Graeme Le Saux: Meadow Lane, Notts County
Nigel Spackman: Plough Lane, Wimbledon
Graham Stuart: Meadow Lane, Notts County
Andy Townsend: Boundary Lane, Oldham
Dennis Wise: McCain Stadium, Scarborough

— ALBERT'S LONG WAIT —

Albert Tennant signed professional terms with Chelsea in November 1934 but, amazingly, didn't make his first-team debut until 12 years later. Before the war Tennant only played reserve-team football for the Blues, while the wartime matches he played in for the club don't count as official games. So, it wasn't until January 1946 that Tennant became a fully-fledged Blue when he appeared in the FA Cup against Leicester City at Stamford Bridge.

— 10-GOAL THRILLERS —

Chelsea and West Ham fans enjoyed a pre-Christmas treat on 17 December 1966 when they watched their teams share 10 goals in a remarkable 5–5 draw at Stamford Bridge. On target for the Blues in the crazy goal-fest were Tommy Baldwin, Tony Hateley, Charlie Cooke and Bobby Tambling (2).

The only other occasion the Blues have been involved in a 5–5 draw was on 30 October 1937 in a match against Bolton at Burnden Park, inside forward Jimmy Argue hitting a hat-trick for the Londoners. The 38,171 fans who turned up at Stamford Bridge for the return fixture between the clubs later in the season must have been smacking their lips in anticipation of another goal-filled afternoon. Sadly, they were disappointed as the match finished in a 0–0 draw.

— CHAMPIONS LEAGUE GLORY... WRITTEN IN THE STARS? —

The Blues went into the 2012 Champions League final as massive underdogs, mainly because they were playing on the home ground of their opponents, Bayern Munich. However, for superstitious Chelsea fans there were a number of omens that suggested the Londoners would prevail against the odds:

- Three previous finals had been played in Munich and on each occasion a new name had been inscribed on the trophy: Nottingham Forest in 1979, Marseille in 1993 and Borussia Dortmund in 1997.
- The last four Champions League/European Cup finals between English and German teams had all been won by the English side: Manchester United beat Bayern 2–1 in 1999, Aston Villa beat Bayern 1–0 in 1981, Nottingham Forest beat Hamburg 1–0 in 1980 and Liverpool beat Borussia Monchengladbach 3–1 in 1977.
- The referee selected for the final, Portugal's Pedro Proenca, had previously officiated at two Bayern matches in the Champions League and on both occasions the Germans had lost: 3–2 at home to Inter Milan in 2011 and 2–0 at home to Bordeaux in 2009.

— MYSTERY OF THE WEATHER VANE —

In the early 1930s a weather vane, depicting a player said to be George Hilsdon, was put up on Chelsea's original East Stand. Over time a superstition developed among some fans that Chelsea's fortunes would plummet if the weather vane was ever taken down.

However, in 1972 the weather vane had to be removed when the old East Stand was demolished. Weather-beaten and rusty, the vane was sent for extensive repairs to a specialist ironworks in the Midlands. Predictably, according to some at least, Chelsea immediately entered a dark period of financial chaos, falling crowds, rampant hooliganism and depressing results culminating in relegation to the Second Division. The curse of the missing vane had struck.

Even the ironworks, where the model of Hilsdon lay rusting in a pile of scrap, went bankrupt. When Ken Bates became Chelsea chairman in 1982 he was told of the curse and swiftly ordered a new vane to take the place of the original. This was promptly restored to the top of the old West Stand and, within a short time, the Blues' fortunes took a distinct turn for the better, with the club gaining promotion back to the First Division in 1984.

— MANAGERS' RECORDS IN EUROPE —

Fourteen Chelsea managers have pitted their wits against the continent's finest in European competition, and generally they have done pretty well. Their respective records (below) reveal that Roberto Di Matteo, who led the Blues to victory in the Champions League in 2012, is the most successful while Avram Grant, who guided Chelsea to their first Champions League Final in 2008, figures higher up the list than his predecessor in the Bridge hotseat, Jose Mourinho:

	P	W	D	L	F	A	Success %
Roberto di Matteo	6	4	2	0	11	5	83%
Dave Sexton	18	11	6	1	48	10	78%
Ruud Gullit	4	3	0	1	13	4	75%
Ted Drake	4	3	0	1	9	6	75%
Avram Grant	12	6	5	1	20	8	71%
Gianluca Vialli	30	17	7	6	45	23	68%
Luiz Felipe Scolari	6	3	2	1	9	5	67%
Guus Hiddink	6	2	4	0	11	8	67%
Carlo Ancelotti	18	10	3	5	29	14	64%
Claudio Ranieri	21	11	5	5	31	20	64%
Jose Mourinho	33	16	9	8	50	27	62%
Andre Villas-Boas	7	3	2	2	14	7	57%
Glenn Hoddle	8	3	3	2	10	8	56%
Tommy Docherty	12	5	3	4	15	15	54%

— RON'S DOUBLE HEADER —

When some players complain about having to play twice a week they are unlikely to get any sympathy from Chelsea legend Ron Harris – he once played two games for the Blues on the same day! In the morning of 4 September 1977 'Chopper' turned out for Chelsea reserves, playing 90 minutes of a 1–0 defeat of Crystal Palace at Stamford Bridge. He then dashed over to The Den, where he was substitute for the first team fixture at Millwall. At half-time, with the Blues trailing 3–0, Ron came on for the injured Steve Finnieston and played the whole of a goalless second half.

— ENGLAND AT THE BRIDGE —

Four full England internationals have been played at Stamford Bridge, the home side winning all of the games. Forget the new Wembley, perhaps England should set up home at the Bridge:

Year	Result
1913	England 1 Scotland 0
1929	England 6 Wales 0
1932	England 4 Austria 3
1946	England 4 Switzerland 1

— BOO BOY TARGETS —

While most Chelsea players have enjoyed a good relationship with the Stamford Bridge crowd, a handful have suffered from barracking from a section of supporters. Players to be on the wrong end of the boo boys' taunts include:

Peter Houseman (1963–75): the left-winger, dubbed 'Mary' by some fans, lacked the glamour possessed by some of his team-mates, while occasional rumours that the iconic George Best was set to join Chelsea from Manchester United didn't help his cause.

Graham Wilkins (1972–82): a loyal Chelsea servant for a decade, Graham was nonetheless compared unfavourably to his much more illustrious brother, Ray. An unfortunate series of own goals didn't do much to endear him to the fans, either.

Paul Canoville (1982–86): a pacy left-winger who contributed some valuable goals in the Blues' 1983/84 promotion campaign, Canoville was disgracefully booed by some fans simply for being black.

Darren Wood (1984–89): a versatile player who could do a job in both defence or midfield, Wood became a target for the terrace snipers when he was picked ahead of the more flamboyant and creative Mick Hazard.

Dave Beasant (1989–92): initially hailed as 'England's Number One', the fans turned on Beasant after a series of high profile boobs cost Chelsea dearly.

Slavisa Jokanovic (2000–02): a methodical but somewhat ponderous midfielder, Claudio Ranieri's first signing never won over the fans and by the end of his stay in West London the simple announcement of Jokanovic's name could be guaranteed to generate a resounding chorus of boos.

— DESERT ISLAND BLUE —

Known to many as the co-writer of popular sitcoms *Drop the Dead Donkey* and *Outnumbered*, Andy Hamilton is also a huge Chelsea fan. In April 1997 he appeared on *Desert Island Discs* and proudly revealed his support for the Blues to the listening millions by choosing *Blue is the Colour* as one of his eight favourite songs. "It was between this and a bit of Verdi," the pint-sized comedy writer told presenter Sue Lawley, "but in the end I had to go for this because I am genetically afflicted with being a Chelsea fan, having been born two minutes' walk from the ground." It was the first time that a 'castaway' had chosen *Blue is the Colour*, the Chelsea anthem taking its place on the show alongside Hamilton's other selections, which included *Sloop John B* by The Beach Boys, *Uptown Girl* by Billy Joel and the Motown classic *Dancing in the Street* by Martha Reeves and The Vandellas.

— SUPERSUBS —

Ivorian strikers Didier Drogba and Salomon Kalou jointly hold the club record for the most goals by a Chelsea substitute, with 14 apiece.

Mikael Forssell is another player with an excellent record as a substitute. In January 2002 the Finn scored in four consecutive games – against Bolton, Norwich, West Ham and Tottenham – after coming off the bench each time. Almost as impressively, his total playing time during the four matches was just 89 minutes. In the whole of the 2001/02 season Forssell scored nine goals for the Blues as a sub, setting another club record.

— FA PREMIER LEAGUE MANAGER OF THE MONTH —

Inaugurated at the start of the 1993/94 season, this award has been won ten times by a Chelsea manager:

Month	Manager
September 2003	Claudio Ranieri
March 2004	Claudio Ranieri
November 2004	Jose Mourinho
January 2005	Jose Mourinho
March 2007	Jose Mourinho
April 2008	Avram Grant
November 2009	Carlo Ancelotti
August 2010	Carlo Ancelotti
March 2011	Carlo Ancelotti
April 2011	Carlo Ancelotti

— WILL WE WIN AGAIN? —

In season 1987/88 Chelsea went 21 league games without a win, the worst such run in the club's history. The dismal sequence began on 3 November 1987 with a 3–1 defeat away to Arsenal and continued until 9 April 1988 when a Mickey Hazard goal gave the Blues all three points at home to Derby County. The record-breaking run cost manager John Hollins his job and was largely responsible for the Blues' ultimate fate – relegation to the Second Division after a play-off defeat by Middlesbrough.

— CHAMPIONS IN THE END —

As the pundits never tire of reminding us, the league season is a marathon and not a sprint. Just as well, really, for Chelsea's championship-winning side of 1955 as for much of the campaign they looked unlikely title contenders. Here's how the Blues' league position fluctuated over the course of a memorable season:

Month (end)	Position in table
August	6th
September	3rd
October	12th
November	11th
December	5th
January	6th
February	3rd
March	1st
April	1st

— WHO THE BLEEDIN' HELL ARE YOU? —

Some unlikely figures have pulled on the famous Blues shirt over the years, including:

- Scouse comedian (and Liverpool fan) Jimmy Tarbuck came on as a substitute for Alan Birchenall in Ken Shellito's testimonial against QPR at Stamford Bridge on 6 May 1968. History doesn't record how the tubby comic fared, but Chelsea manager Dave Sexton was clearly insufficiently impressed to sign Tarby up for the following season.
- Ten years later, on 27 November 1978, fans in the Shed were rubbing their eyes with disbelief when Capital Radio DJs Dave Cash and Graham Dene played the second half for Chelsea against QPR. OK, it was only another testimonial game – this time for Blues long-throw

legend and 1970 FA Cup winner Ian Hutchinson – but Rangers seemed to be taking the game somewhat more seriously . . . their two subs were England internationals Ian Gillard and Clive Allen!

- The manager of the Chelsea restaurant, Leon Lenik, swapped his dinner jacket for a football shirt to come on as a substitute for Colin Pates in Mickey Droy's testimonial match against Arsenal at Stamford Bridge on 1 November 1983. The Blues won the game 2–1, with Droy scoring one of the home team's goals.

- On 14 May 1984 Chelsea programme editor Hugh Hastings replaced Kerry Dixon in a testimonial match for Brentford's Eddie Lyons at Griffin Park. Hastings, it has to be said, didn't quite live up to the standard set by Dixon who had scored five goals by the time he was substituted. Chelsea won the match 6–3.

- Another non-footballer to get a run out for the Blues is former Chelsea masseur and diehard fan Terry Byrne. Terry came on for Frank Leboeuf towards the end of the Blues' 6–0 tour match defeat of Brunei in May 1997 and, by all accounts, acquitted himself well. Nonetheless, then boss Ruud Gullit resisted the temptation to promote him to the first-team squad.

- Finally, fitness trainer Antonio Pintus replaced Bjarne Goldbaek for the last five minutes of the Blues' match against Instant District of Hong Kong in May 1999. Chelsea won the game 2–1.

— ALL CHANGE —

On two occasions in Chelsea's history a completely different team has lined up for the Blues in successive matches. On 13 October 1999 Gianluca Vialli chose the following 11 players for the Worthington Cup third round tie against Huddersfield at Stamford Bridge: Cudicini; Lambourde, Terry, Hogh, Le Saux; Goldbaek, Morris, Di Matteo, Ambrosetti; Flo, Forssell. Three days later, the Chelsea team which faced Liverpool at Anfield showed 11 changes and lined up as follows: De Goey; Ferrer, Desailly, Leboeuf, Babayaro; Petrescu, Deschamps, Wise, Poyet; Sutton, Zola. Unfortunately for Vialli, his rotation policy was unsuccessful as the Blues lost both games 1–0.

Then, in 2008, Avram Grant made similar use of his large squad, selecting two distinct starting XIs for consecutive matches against Huddersfield in the FA Cup fifth round and against Olympiakos in the Champions League. Against the League One side on 16 February, Grant put out the following team: Cudicini; Ferreira, Terry, Ben Haim, Bridge; Mikel, Sidwell, Lampard; Sinclair, Pizarro, Kalou. In Athens three days later it was all change, as the Israeli opted for this side: Cech; Belletti, Alex, Carvalho, A. Cole; Makelele, Essien, Ballack; J. Cole, Drogba,

Malouda. Grant's results proved better than Vialli's, with the Blues recording a win and a draw in the two games.

— ADVERTISING HEAVEN —

There may not have been any company logos on the players' shirts, but the 1970s was the heyday of perimeter board advertising. Here's just a selection of the ads on show around the ground at Stamford Bridge for the match between Chelsea and Manchester United on 28 April 1973:

Bostik
Bovril
Cecil Gee Menswear
Chelsea Building Society
Coca Cola
Drink Young's Bitter
Duckhams
Evening Standard, The Greatest London Paper
Fly Lufthansa International
Ford
Fyffes
Go Esso . . . Buy Esso . . . Drive Esso
Laing, Construction On Time
Levi's
Power Sportshoes
Puma
SKF Bearings
Stone's Ginger Wine
Stylo Matchmakers
Sun Alliance
Van Heusen Shirts
White Horse Scotch Whisky

— THE SAYINGS OF JOSE MOURINHO —

"We have top players and, sorry if I'm arrogant, we have a top manager. Please don't call me arrogant, but I'm European champion and I think I'm a special one." **Shortly after being appointed Chelsea manager, July 2004**

"My philosophy in football is that there is only one winner. The second is the first of the last." **Revealing his ultra-competitive streak, July 2004**

"As we say in Portugal, they bought the bus and they left the bus in front of the goal." **After Tottenham had packed their defence to gain a 0–0 draw at the Bridge, September 2004**

"Maybe when I turn 60 and have been managing in the same league for 20 years I'll have the respect of everybody, I'll have the power to speak to people and make them tremble a bit." **Accusing Sir Alex Ferguson of influencing the referee, January 2005**

"In football, top people are never scared. We always want to play against the big teams, the big managers; players always want to play big players." **After the Champions League draw paired Chelsea with Barcelona, December 2004**

"Defeat in the first leg is not a defeat. We are just losing at half-time." **Looking on the bright side, before the Champions League last 16 second leg with Barcelona, March 2005**

"What honeymoon? The only honeymoon I have had is the 20 years with my wife." **Responding to the question 'Is the honeymoon over?' after two defeats on the trot, February 2005**

"I'm feeling a lot of pressure with the problem in Scotland. Football is nothing compared with life. For me bird flu is the drama of the last few days. I'll have to buy a mask." **More worried about bird flu than Manchester United's ultimately futile title challenge, April 2006**

"I think it would be difficult for anyone to be manager of any club after me. I wouldn't recommend it."
Fully aware that he's a tough act to follow, January 2007

"You show when you are happy, you show when you are not happy. Sometimes you kiss [the players], sometimes you kick."
On his management style, January 2007

"In the supermarket you have class one, two or class three eggs and some are more expensive than others and give you better omelettes. So when the class one eggs are in Waitrose and you cannot go there, you have a problem." **Bemoaning the lack of money spent on new signings, September 2007**

"There are only two ways for me to leave Chelsea. One is in June 2010, when I finish my contract. If the club does not give me a new one it is the end of my contract and I am out. The second way is for Chelsea to sack me because there's not a third way."
Denying reports that he might leave Chelsea of his own accord, February 2007

"Who am I to question the owner of the club? Abramovich is all-powerful at Chelsea."
Acknowledging his subordinate position in Chelsea's hierarchy, March 2007

— 2004/05: A RECORD-BREAKING SEASON —

Chelsea's championship-winning side of 2004/05 not only won the title at a canter but also set a number of significant top flight, Premiership and club records, including:

- The Blues' total of 95 points is an all-time top-flight record. Manchester United previously held the record with 92 points in their first 'Double' season, 1993/94.
- Chelsea's goals against tally of just 15 equalled Preston's record, set in the Football League's first season, 1888/89. However, Preston only played 22 games and the previous record for fewest goals conceded

in a League campaign was usually previously credited to Liverpool (16 goals conceded in 42 games in 1978/79).

- In the second half of the season Chelsea won nine consecutive away league games, setting a new top flight record for English football. The record stood until 2008, when the Blues picked up all three points in 11 consecutive Premier League away games.
- During the 2004/05 season the Blues recorded 10 consecutive clean sheets in the Premiership, setting another all-time top flight record. The previous best of eight was jointly held by Liverpool (1922/23) and Arsenal (1998/99).
- Eight consecutive Premiership wins all with clean sheets equalled an all-time European top flight record held jointly by Partizan Belgrade and Skonto Riga.
- Chelsea's total of 25 clean sheets in the League set a new Premiership record, surpassing Manchester United's 24 in 1994/95. However, Liverpool retain the all-time top flight record with 28 clean sheets in 1978/79.
- Chelsea's record of just one league defeat in a league campaign is a club record and has only ever been surpassed in the top flight by Preston (1888/89) and Arsenal (2003/04), both of whom went through a whole league season unbeaten.
- The Blues' goal difference of +57 was the best in the club's history at the time, until Carlo Ancelotti's Double winners posted a goal difference of +71 in 2009/10.
- Throughout the 2004/05 season Chelsea suffered just six defeats, equalling a club record established in 1998/99. The only sides to beat Mourinho's Blues were Manchester City (Premiership), Newcastle (FA Cup) and Porto, Barcelona, Bayern Munich and Liverpool in the Champions League.
- 12 league doubles – against Manchester United, Everton, Liverpool, Middlesbrough, Charlton, Blackburn, Portsmouth, Fulham, West Bromwich Albion, Crystal Palace, Norwich and Southampton – created a new club record, beating the eight the Blues managed in 1906/07 and 1962/63.
- Goalkeeper Petr Cech set a new club record of 28 clean sheets, beating Ed de Goey's previous record of 27 in season 1999/2000. Altogether, Chelsea recorded 34 clean sheets, another club record.
- The Blues' total of 15 away league victories set a new club record, beating the previous best of 14 in the old Second Division in 1988/89.
- Chelsea's total of 42 games won in all competitions set yet another club record, beating the previous best of 36 wins in 2003/04.

— 16-GOAL EXTRAVAGANZA —

On 29 November 1966 Chelsea played a London XI, featuring such legendary names as Bobby Robson, Johnny Haynes and England World Cup winner George Cohen, in a testimonial match for the Blues' long-serving defender John Mortimore. The final score was 9–7 to Chelsea, making this the highest-scoring match the Blues have ever been involved in. The 16 strikes were neatly divided between the first and second halves, and worked out on average at a goal every five minutes and 37 seconds.

— IT'S A SQUAD GAME NOW —

Since substitutes were first introduced into English football at the start of the 1965/66 season, the number of subs Chelsea have used over the course of a campaign has been steadily rising. Claudio Ranieri was the first Blues boss to make more than a century of substitutions in a Premiership season, with 102 in 2000/01. Jose Mourinho set a new high with 111 changes in 2004/05, before beating his own record with 113 substitutions out of a possible 114 the following season – the only time he failed to use his full complement of three subs was during the 2–0 victory against Arsenal at Highbury in December 2005. By way of contrast, Eddie McCreadie made just seven substitutions during the whole of the Blues' 1976/77 promotion campaign.

— CHELSEA UP, TOTTENHAM DOWN —

Blues fans had smiles as wide as the Grand Canyon in May 1977 when Chelsea were promoted to the First Division while hated rivals Tottenham moved in the opposite direction, slipping into the Second Division for the first time since 1950. However, Spurs bounced back the following season and have maintained their top-flight status ever since; Chelsea, on the other hand, have suffered two subsequent relegations.

— OUCH! THAT HURT —

A number of Chelsea players have collected injuries in unusual circumstances. These include:

- **John Boyle:** The Blues' midfielder was knocked unconscious when he was struck by a bottle thrown by a Roma fan during Chelsea's Fairs Cup match with the Italians in Rome on 6 October 1965. However, Boyle, a tough Scotsman, recovered to play on in the match which ended in a 0–0 draw.

- **Alan Hudson:** The teenage prodigy missed the 1970 FA Cup Final after injuring his ankle in a freak incident during a game at West Brom. "There was nobody near me when it happened," he said later. "I just landed badly, my foot went down a hole and that was it. I knew as soon as it happened that it was serious because I was in unbelievable pain." In an effort to get fit for the Blues' Wembley showdown with Leeds, Huddy visited a spiritualist in Victoria. "It was like a palm reading, only she 'read' the bottom of my foot," he recalled. "I was just laughing while she did it and thinking, 'This ain't gonna work'." He was right – it didn't.

- **Steve Kember:** Midfielder Steve had already damaged his front teeth when he was kicked in the face by Ron 'Chopper' Harris while playing against the Blues for Crystal Palace in 1971. He moved to Chelsea later the same year and in 1973 suffered a second unintentional whack in the face from another Blues player. "Playing for Chelsea against Leeds, I went round Paul Madeley one side and Peter Osgood went round him the other," he recalled. "As I've gone to tackle Madeley, Ossie accidentally kicked me in the face and knocked my teeth out again." Painful.

- **Dave Beasant:** In the summer of 1993 goalkeeper Dave was making lunch at home when he knocked a bottle of salad cream off the kitchen work surface. Attempting to prevent the bottle smashing on the floor, Beasant tried to control it with his foot but only succeeded in rupturing ligaments in his ankle. He was sidelined for two months, and didn't play another match for the Blues before joining Southampton.

- **Carlo Cudicini:** The Italian goalkeeper injured himself while taking his dog for a walk in the summer of 2001 and was eventually forced to have minor surgery on his knee. "I don't know whether his dog is a Rottweiler or a Pekinese," Chelsea assistant manager Gwyn Williams told reporters, "but Carlo was out walking it and it must have seen a rabbit or something because it gave him a sharp tug. Carlo felt his knee tweak. He thought it was alright but, a bit later, it was still giving him problems." The bizarre injury kept Cudicini out of the Blues' team until the autumn, although he recovered sufficiently to win the club's Player of the Year award by the end of the campaign.

— PRESENT AND CORRECT —

The following three players played in every league game during one of Chelsea's four title-winning seasons:

Season	Player	League matches played
1954/55	Eric Parsons	42
1954/55	Derek Saunders	42
2004/05	Frank Lampard	38

— TWO FEMALE FIRSTS —

Sharon Rivers made history on 5 December 1994 when she became the first woman to officiate in a match at Stamford Bridge, running the line in an FA Youth Cup second round replay between Chelsea and Leyton Orient. Maybe the young Blues, who included future first team players Jody Morris and Mark Nicholls, found her presence distracting as they lost the match 2–0.

In 1989 Yvonne Todd became the first female member of the board of directors of Chelsea FC. She served on the board until 2003.

— MONEY TOO TIGHT TO MENTION —

Between July 1974, when David Hay arrived from Celtic for £225,000, and September 1978, when the Blues bought Duncan McKenzie from Everton for £165,000, Chelsea did not spend a penny on player purchases. This four-year unofficial 'transfer embargo' was a product of the massive debts – £3.4 million at one point – the club accumulated following the building of the East Stand. With no money to spend on transfer fees, Chelsea instead had to rely on their youth system – so much so that of the 20 players used during the 1976/77 promotion season no fewer than 15 were former members of the youth team. Remarkably, in four games of that same season the eleven players Chelsea fielded had not cost the club a single penny in transfer fees.

— THE THREE AMIGOS —

The first time Chelsea fielded three players from the same country outside the British isles are as follows:

Date	Players	Nationality	Result
16 Nov 1996	Roberto di Matteo Gianluca Vialli Gianfranco Zola	Italian	Blackburn 1 Chelsea 1
9 Sept 1998	Marcel Desailly Bernard Lambourde Frank Leboeuf	French	Chelsea 0 Arsenal 0
13 Aug 2000	Ed de Goey JF Hasselbaink Mario Melchiot	Dutch	Chelsea 2 Manchester United 0
21 Aug 2004	Ricardo Carvalho Paulo Ferreira Tiago	Portuguese	Birmingham 0 Chelsea 1
9 April 2011	Alex David Luiz Ramires	Brazilian	Chelsea 1 Wigan 0
10 Sept 2011	Juan Mata Oriol Romeu Fernando Torres	Spanish	Sunderland 1 Chelsea 2

— TIME WARP —

On 27 December 1986 Chelsea fans were stunned to discover that, according to the front cover of the matchday programme at least, that afternoon's home game against Aston Villa was taking place on 'Saturday 27th December 1968'. It was just a misprint, of course, but happily the Blues – struggling at the foot of the First Division at the time – showed some of their goal-filled 60s form by thrashing Villa 4–1.

— TWO TV FIRSTS —

- These days Chelsea feature in more live TV matches than just about any English team. But that wasn't always the case. Indeed, it wasn't until May 1984 that the Blues first appeared in a live league game, the BBC covering their visit to Manchester City in the old Second Division. Chelsea delighted their armchair fans by winning the match 2–0, the goals coming from Pat Nevin and Kerry Dixon.
- The first Chelsea Premiership match to be shown live on Sky was the Blues' visit to Manchester City (again) on Sunday 20 September 1992. The game didn't quite live up to Sky's 'Super Sunday' hype, but Chelsea fans were more than pleased with a 1–0 win thanks to Mick Harford's goal.

— SPECIAL GOAL —

Roberto di Matteo scores after 43 seconds

In 2004 the official Chelsea magazine asked readers to vote for the most important goal in the club's history. Once the votes had been added up, the top five goals were:

1) Roberto di Matteo, v Middlesbrough, 1997 FA Cup Final   33%
2) Jesper Gronkjaer, v Liverpool, Premiership 2003   19%
3) David Webb, v Leeds United, 1970 FA Cup Final replay   18%
4) Mark Hughes, v Vicenza, 1998 ECWC semi-final second leg   9%
5) Wayne Bridge, v Arsenal, 2004 Champions League, quarter-final   8%

— LET THERE BE LIGHT —

The first match to be staged under floodlights at Stamford Bridge was a friendly against Czech side Sparta Prague on 19 March 1957. Six floodlights (a number only matched at the time by Hull City), each 170 feet high, and costing a total of £37,000 illuminated proceedings as the Blues won 2–0 with goals by Les Allen and Derek Gibbs. The experiment was a success with the fans, too, attracting a crowd of 30,701 to the Bridge.

— BLUE TAXI —

Hail a black cab in London and the chances are that the driver will be an ex-Chelsea player. Among the former Blues to have passed 'the Knowledge' are Gary Chivers, John Bumstead, Alan Dickens, Trevor Aylott and Mickey Hazard. No doubt, the lads would appreciate a decent tip if you do happen to make use of their services.

— CHELSEA MANAGERS —

The full list of Blues bosses, along with the silverware they deposited in the Bridge trophy cabinet:

Manager	Years	Trophies Won
John Tait Robertson	1905–06	-
William Lewis	1906–07	-
David Calderhead	1907–33	-
Leslie Knighton	1933–39	-
Billy Birrell	1939–52	-
Ted Drake	1952–61	League Championship (1955), Charity Shield (1955)
Tommy Docherty	1961–67	League Cup (1965)
Dave Sexton	1967–74	FA Cup (1970), European Cup Winners Cup (1971)
Ron Suart	1974–75	-
Eddie McCreadie	1975–77	-
Ken Shellito	1977–78	-
Danny Blanchflower	1978–79	-
Geoff Hurst	1979–81	-
John Neal	1981–85	Second Division Championship (1984)
John Hollins	1985–88	Full Members Cup (1986)
Bobby Campbell	1988–91	Second Division Championship (1989), ZDS Cup (1990)

Ian Porterfield	1991–93	-
David Webb	1993	-
Glenn Hoddle	1993–96	-
Ruud Gullit	1996–98	FA Cup (1997)
Gianluca Vialli	1998–2000	Coca-Cola Cup (1998), European Cup Winners Cup (1998), European Super Cup (1998), FA Cup (2000), Charity Shield (2000)
Claudio Ranieri	2000–04	-
Jose Mourinho	2004–07	Carling Cup (2005, 2007) Premiersh League (2005, 2006) Community Shield (2005), FA Cup (2007)
Avram Grant	2007–08	-
Luiz Felipe Scolari	2008–09	-
Guus Hiddink	2009	FA Cup (2009)
Carlo Ancelotti	2009–11	Community Shield (2009), Premier League (2010), FA Cup (2010)
Andre Villas-Boas	2011–12	-
Roberto di Matteo	2012	FA Cup (2012), Champions League (2012)

— A TV RECORD —

The 1970 FA Cup Final replay between Chelsea and Leeds at Old Trafford attracted the largest ever television audience for a domestic match, with more than 28 million viewers tuning in to the live coverage on the BBC and ITV channels. Incredibly, the combined audience figure for the match puts it in the all-time top 10 of British TV ratings successes:

1.	World Cup Final (1966)	32.3 million
2.	Princess Diana's funeral (1997)	32.1 million
3.	*EastEnders* (Den and Ange divorce episode, 1986)	31.15 million
4.	Royal Family documentary (1969)	30.69 million
5.	Apollo 13 splashdown (1970)	28.6 million
6.	Chelsea v Leeds, FA Cup Final replay (1970)	28.49 million
7.	Charles and Diana wedding (1981)	28.4 million
8.	Princess Anne's wedding (1973)	27.6 million

9. *Coronation Street* (Blackpool tram   26.93 million
    horror episode, 1989)
10. Royal Variety Show (1965)   24.2 million

— POMPEY PURPLE PATCH —

The team the Blues enjoy playing most is Portsmouth. It's now 48 years since Pompey last beat Chelsea (1–0 in a League Cup tie in December 1960). Since then the Pompey chimes have been distinctly muted, as in 31 meetings between the sides in all competitions, the Blues have notched up 24 wins and seven draws, scoring 76 goals and conceding just 16.

— DARLING, YOU WERE MARVELLOUS! —

Partly because of Stamford Bridge's location a short distance away from the West End, Chelsea have always been popular among showbiz types. In the 1960s and 1970s famous names such as Sean Connery, Michael Caine, John Cleese, Tom Courtneay, Michael Crawford and Dennis Waterman were regular visitors to the Bridge, while American superstars Raquel Welch and Steve McQueen also saw the Blues in action. Veteran luvvie Lord (Richard) Attenborough, of course, has a long association with Chelsea and is now the club's Life Vice President, having previously been a director. Actors who regularly attend Chelsea matches these days include Clive Mantle, Phil Daniels and Trevor Eve.

— FRANK'S DREAM TEAM —

In December 2011 Frank Lampard was asked by www.theguardian.co.uk to select his all-time favourite five-a-side team, choosing from the players he has played with during his long career. Here are his picks, which include four current or former Chelsea players:

Petr Cech: "I'd have Petr Cech in goal. He's been so consistent over all the years I've played with him. The one 'keeper who'd rival him is Joe Hart, but as I haven't played so long with Harty I'll go for Petr."

John Terry: "JT is a defender who would be inspirational and tough, and he's a quality player as we all know. I've been very lucky to have played with him for such a long time and he walks into the team, basically."

Claude Makelele: "Makelele and John would be the defensive part of the team. He was very under-rated, but the people who've played with him and the fans who watched him at the clubs he played for understand his importance and know what a great link he was between defence and attack."

Gianfranco Zola: "Franco has been a big influence on my career. He's an amazing player and an amazing personality. At five-a-side he would be fantastic because he's got that close control and one or two-touch finish. He came back to train with us a couple of years after he'd finished playing, when he about 40 years old, and he still had that sharpness about him."

Gianfranco Zola: an amazing player

Wayne Rooney: "He's been pretty much the outstanding player I've played with in the England squad. He's got that ability to make things happen, similar to Franco Zola."

— POINT OF ORDER, MR REFEREE! —

Chelsea enjoy good support on both sides of the House in the Commons and the Lords. Former or current politicians who follow the Blues include:

Sir John Major	(Former Conservative Prime Minister)
David Mellor	(Former Conservative MP for Putney)
Sebastian Coe	(Former Conservative MP for Falmouth and Cambourne, now Lord Coe of Ranmore)
Peter Bottomley	(Conservative MP for Worthing West)
George Osbourne	(Chancellor of the Exchequer and Conservative MP for Tatton)
Peter Hain	(Labour MP for Neath)
Hugh Robertson	(Minister for Sport and Conservative MP for Faversham and Mid Kent)
Ed Vaizey	(Minister for Culture, Communications and Creative Industries and Conservative MP for Wantage)

— CUP WINNING BOSSES —

In the early 1990s Chelsea had a trio of managers who shared one thing in common: they had all scored winning goals in the FA Cup Final. Ian Porterfield (manager from 1991–93) had scored Sunderland's winner when they beat Leeds in the 1973 final, while caretaker boss Dave Webb (1993) had, of course, clinched victory for the Blues, again over Leeds, in 1970. Webb's replacement, Glenn Hoddle (1993–96), was another Wembley hero having scored the winner for Spurs in the FA Cup Final replay against QPR in 1982. The unusual sequence ended when Ruud Gullit took over from Hoddle in 1996, although he ended up leading the Blues to FA Cup Final glory the following year.

— WE HATE ARSENAL . . . AND TOTTENHAM . . . AND MAN U! —

In 2004 the website Planetfootball.com carried out a survey of fans around the country, asking them to name the club they considered to be their team's biggest rival. Among Chelsea fans, Arsenal (1st), Tottenham (2nd) and Manchester United (3rd) headed the list.

Meanwhile, Chelsea were considered to be important rivals by fans of Fulham (1st), QPR (1st), Leeds (2nd), Arsenal (3rd), Tottenham (3rd) and West Ham (3rd).

— SMALL SQUAD PAYS DIVIDENDS —

In 1970 Chelsea used just 13 players during their successful FA Cup run (compared to 18 in 1997, 22 in 2000, 24 in 2007, 25 in 2009, 23 in 2010 and 21 in 2012). Of these, seven players – Peter Bonetti, John Dempsey, John Hollins, Peter Houseman, Ian Hutchinson, Eddie McCreadie and David Webb – were on the field for all 810 minutes of cup football. Skipper Ron Harris also started all eight FA Cup games but, feeling the effects of an injury, was substituted at the start of extra-time against Leeds in the final at Wembley.

— GEORGE'S GLORIOUS GOAL —

On 12 January 2000 former World Player of the Year George Weah made a dramatic entrance on to the Chelsea scene, coming off the bench to score a late winner for the Blues against London rivals Tottenham. In just a matter of minutes he had become a cult hero for the Bridge fans, and one of just eight players to have scored on their Chelsea debuts as a substitute. Here's the full list:

Year	Player	Player Replaced	Result
1980	Chris Hutchings	Mike Fillery	Cardiff 0 Chelsea 1
1988	David Lee	Darren Wood	Chelsea 2 Leicester 1
1991	Joe Allon	Kevin Wilson	Chelsea 2 Wibledon 2
1992	Eddie Newton	Graeme Le Saux	Everton 2 Chelsea 1
1997	Paul Hughes	Dennis Wise	Chelsea 3 Derby 1
1997	Tore Andre Flo	Mark Hughes	Coventry 3 Chelsea 2
2000	George Weah	Gus Poyet	Chelsea 1 Tottenham 0
2011	Juan Mata	Florent Malouda	Chelsea 3 Norwich City 1

— JIMMY'S QUICK-FIRE HAT-TRICK —

Goal grabber extraordinaire Jimmy Floyd Hasselbaink is the only Chelsea player to have scored a hat-trick after coming on as a sub. Jimmy notched his three goals in a 13-minute spell in the 5–2 defeat of Wolves at Stamford Bridge on 27 March 2004.

A further ten players have scored twice for the Blues as a sub, including lanky Norwegian striker Tore Andre Flo who achieved this feat on two occasions in 1998, at home to Crystal Palace (won 6–2) and away to Blackburn (won 4–3).

— LUNG TONIC? THAT'S JUST WHAT I NEED . . . —

Sample ads from the Chelsea FC official handbook of 1910:

"Hand-made football boots. As supplied to Chelsea, Tottenham, Fulham, Queens Park Rangers, Crystal Palace, Brentford, and many leading amateur clubs. 12/6." **T.C. Gill, boot makers, Middlesbrough**

"All Chelsea matches are criticised fairly and fearlessly in *The Daily Chronicle*." ***The Daily Chronicle* newspaper**

"Green & London for footballs by best makers. Within a stone's throw of these grounds." **Green & London, Walham Green**

"At the first sign of cold or chill, take Owbridge's lung tonic. Beware of substitutes. Football spectators run greater risks than players." **Owbridge's lung tonic**

— WHO'S IN GOAL THIS WEEK? —

Chelsea boss Ruud Gullit helped to set a club record in season 1996/97 by selecting no fewer than five different goalkeepers at one time or another during the campaign. Norwegian international keeper Frode Grodas headed the list with 26 and one sub appearances, followed by Kevin Hitchcock (10 and two sub), Dmitri Kharine (5), on loan goalie Craig Forrest (2 and one sub) and Nick Colgan (one appearance). Presumably, though, Gullit was not especially impressed by any of the quintet as in the summer of 1997 he splashed out £2.25 million to bring Dutch international keeper Ed de Goey to Stamford Bridge.

— AWAYDAY BLUES —

1993 was a grim year to follow Chelsea away from home as, incredibly, the Blues failed to record a single victory on opposition soil during the whole calendar year. In all, the Blues played 24 away matches in 1993, losing 16 and drawing eight. The depressing run finally came to an end on New Year's Day 1994 when Chelsea won 3–1 at manager Glenn Hoddle's old club, Swindon Town.

— CUP WINNERS ALL —

A team of Chelsea players who won the FA Cup with a club other than the Blues:

1. Vic Woodley (Derby County, 1946)
2. Vinnie Jones (Wimbledon, 1988)
3. Ashley Cole (Arsenal, 2002, 2003 and 2005)
4. Ray Wilkins (Manchester United, 1983)
5. Graham Roberts (Tottenham, 1981 and 1982)
6. Graham Stuart (Everton, 1995)
7. Jim McCalliog (Southampton, 1976)
8. George Graham (Arsenal, 1971)
9. Jimmy Greaves (Tottenham, 1962 and 1967)
10. Harold Halse (Manchester United, 1909)
11. John Sissons (West Ham United, 1964)
Manager: Ian Porterfield (Sunderland, 1973)

— SCHOOL DAYS —

The schools where a selection of Chelsea players, past and present, first demonstrated their football skills:

Bexley Grammar School, Welling: Gavin Peacock
Brentwood School, Essex: Frank Lampard
Chiswick Community School, west London: Carlton Cole
Eastbury Comprehensive School, Barking: John Terry
Enfield Grammar School, north London: Michael Duberry
Haberdashers' Aske's Hatcham College, New Cross Gate: Scott Parker, Shaun Wright-Phillips
Haverstock Hill School, Camden: Joe Cole
Kings' School, Winchester: Wayne Bridge
St Aloysius RC College, north London: Joe Cole
Sir Christopher Wren School, White City: Dennis Wise
Marlborough School, Woodstock: Josh McEachran

— HOLLY AND FRANKIE'S RECORD RUNS —

Chelsea midfielder John Hollins set a club record in the early 1970s when he appeared in 168 consecutive matches for the Blues. The sequence – which consisted of 135 league games, 10 FA Cup, 19 League Cup and four in the European Cup Winners Cup – began on 14 August 1971 and continued until 25 September 1974.

In season 2005/06 Frank Lampard set a new record for consecutive appearances in the Premiership. When his run came to an end through illness in December 2005 Lampard's total stood at 164, five ahead of David James' previous Premiership record of 159.

Frank Lampard: 168 Chelsea games in a row

— LEAGUE CUP SUCCESS —

The Blues have won the League Cup on four occasions, most recently in 2007 when two Didier Drogba goals saw off Arsenal at the Millennium Stadium in Cardiff. Two years earlier Drogba was on target again as Chelsea defeated Liverpool in the final at the same venue.

The first time the Blues won the competition, in 1965, the final was played over two-legs. After a rare Eddie McCreadie goal secured a 3–2 victory over Leicester at the Bridge, the Blues hung on for a 0–0 draw in the return to take the cup. After a 33-year wait, Chelsea won the League Cup for a second time, extra-time goals from Frank Sinclair and Roberto di Matteo seeing off Middlesbrough.

League Cup Final	Result	Venue
1965	Chelsea 3 Leicester City 2 (agg)	Home/ away
1972	Chelsea 1 Stoke City 2	Wembley
1998 (Coca-Cola Cup)	Chelsea 2 Middlesbrough 0*	Wembley
2005 (Carling Cup)	Chelsea 3 Liverpool 2*	Millennium Stadium
2007 (Carling Cup)	Chelsea 2 Arsenal 1	Millennium Stadium
2008 (Carling Cup)	Chelsea 1 Tottenham 2	Wembley

* After extra-time

— BEN'S SPECIAL GOAL —

Benjamin Howard Baker holds a unique position in Chelsea history as the only goalkeeper to have scored a goal for the club. His moment of glory came at Stamford Bridge on 19 November 1921 when he slotted a penalty past his Bradford City counterpart Jock Ewart for the only goal of the game. Sadly, Ben's penalty-taking antics soon came to an end when he missed the next one against Arsenal and had to race back in a desperate panic to his own penalty area.

Although not counting as official matches, two Chelsea goalkeepers have scored in testimonial games at the Bridge. In April 1969 Blues legend Peter Bonetti netted two penalties against Charlton in Bobby Tambling's testimonial. Twenty-six years later, in March 1995, Dave Beasant came on for Kerry Dixon in the latter's testimonial match against Spurs and scored the final goal in the Blues' 5–1 win.

— PREMIERSHIP CHAMPIONS 2005 —

In season 2004/05 the Blues won their first Premiership title, exactly 50 years after their last championship triumph in 1955. As well as the glory, Chelsea pocketed £9.5 million in prize money for coming first. Here's how the top of the Premiership table looked at the end of the campaign:

	P	W	D	L	F	A	Pts
Chelsea	38	29	8	1	72	15	95
Arsenal	38	25	8	5	87	36	83
Manchester United	38	22	11	5	58	26	77

— GOALKEEPING CRISIS AVERTED —

On two occasions Chelsea have had to play the full 90 minutes with an outfield player in goal and, miraculously, both stand-ins somehow managed to keep a clean sheet. In Chelsea's very first season defender Bob Mackie filled in for regular keeper Willy 'Fatty' Foulke on 28 October 1905 and helped the Blues win 1–0 away to Southern United in the FA Cup.

On 27 December 1971 occasional emergency keeper David Webb donned the green jersey for the visit of Bobby Robson's Ipswich Town, after injuries ruled out Peter Bonetti and John Phillips and third-choice goalkeeper Steve Sherwood failed to arrive at the Bridge in time for kick off. Having knelt down and prayed in front of the Chelsea fans in the Shed, Webb then proceeded to keep the Ipswich strikers at bay for the whole game as Chelsea ran out 2–0 winners.

Other outfield players to have pulled on the gloves for Chelsea for part of a game include Bert Murray, Bill Garner, Tommy Langley, David Speedie, John Coady, Vinnie Jones, Glen Johnson and, most recently, John Terry.

— CAGED IN . . . AND ELECTRIFIED! —

In October 1972, following a series of pitch invasions during the opening game of the season at home to Leeds, Chelsea became the first British club to erect fences inside their ground. Initially, the eight-foot high fences behind both goals were topped with three strands of barbed wire although these were soon removed.

Thirteen years later, after riotous scenes at the Milk Cup semi-final second leg against Sunderland at Stamford Bridge on 4 March 1985, Chelsea chairman Ken Bates ordered fences to be put up in front of the East and West stands as well. Even more controversially, Bates proposed that the tops of all the fences at the ground should be fitted with a 12-volt electric current which would give potential pitch invaders an unpleasant, but non-lethal, shock.

However, Bates' innovative plan to combat hooliganism was vetoed by the Greater London Council. The chairman of the GLC's public service committee summed up the body's opposition to the scheme by saying: "The idea is very unsavoury. The reaction I have had from my colleagues is 'What comes next?' – water cannons, guards, tanks and consultant undertakers to ferry away the dead?"

— STAMFORD BRIDGE: A POTTED HISTORY —

Stamford Bridge has been the home of Chelsea FC since the club was formed in 1905, although the stadium itself dates back to 1877. Over the decades the ground has radically changed in appearance, and now bears no relation to the stadium fans knew as recently as the early 1970s. What hasn't changed, though, is the sense among Chelsea supporters that Stamford Bridge is their much-loved ancestral home. Here are the key dates in the evolution of the stadium:

1877 Stamford Bridge opens to the public as the home of the London Athletic Club.

1904 The Mears brothers, Gus and Joseph, purchase the freehold of the stadium with a view to using it to stage sporting events, including football.

1905 The 5,000 capacity original East Stand is built, along with vast new terraces. Chelsea FC plays its first competitive match at the Bridge, beating Hull City 5–1.

1935 The Shed is erected above the terraces at the Fulham Road End.

1939 The original North Stand, with a capacity of 2,500, is built above the terraces in the north-east corner of the ground.

1966 The original West Stand opens to fans. Built at a cost of £150,000, it consists of 6,300 seats in 35 rows and, at the front, 3,360 bench seats.

1974 The 11,000–capacity East Stand opens, having cost £2 million. Original plans to make it the first phase of a new 60,000 all-seater stadium are shelved.

1975 The North Stand is demolished.

1994 The Shed End terrace is demolished and replaced with a small temporary stand. Later the same year the North Stand (now the Matthew Harding Stand) opens with a capacity of 10,776.

1997 The West Stand is demolished and the new Shed Stand opens.

2001 After a delay of two years due to planning permission not being granted by the local council, the completed West Stand opens. Built at a cost of around £30 million, it can seat 13,500 fans. In total, the redeveloped Stamford Bridge has a capacity of 41,837. In addition, the stadium complex boosts two four-star hotels, five restaurants, conference and banqueting facilities, a nightclub, an underground car park and a health club.

— CUP DOUBLE —

In the 2006/07 season Chelsea became only the third English club after Arsenal (1993) and Liverpool (2001) to win the FA Cup and League (Carling) Cup in the same season. The Blues claimed the first leg of this double by beating Arsenal 2–1 in the Carling Cup Final at the Millennium Stadium, Cardiff, and the second leg was achieved with a 1–0 victory over Manchester United in the FA Cup Final at Wembley Stadium.

— TRANSFER MILESTONES —

Apart from a spell in the 1970s when the club was stone broke, Chelsea have never been shy about splashing the cash in the transfer market. Here are some milestones along the way to the Blues' current most expensive purchase, Fernando Torres.

Year	Player	Fee	Selling Club
1907	Fred Rouse	£1,000	Stoke City
1923	Andy Wilson	£5,000	Middlesbrough
1930	Hughie Gallacher	£10,000	Newcastle United
1966	Tony Hateley	£100,000	Aston Villa
1990	Andy Townsend	£1.2 million	Norwich City
1997	Graeme Le Saux	£5 million	Blackburn
1999	Chris Sutton	£10 million	Blackburn
2005	Michael Essien	£24.4 million	Lyon
2006	Andriy Shevchenko	£30.8 million	AC Milan
2011	Fernando Torres	£50 million	Liverpool

— BLUE SUNDAY —

Chelsea appeared in the first-ever First Division match to be played on a Sunday, losing 1–0 away to Stoke on 27 January 1974. For many years prior to this Football League teams were prohibited from playing on Sundays, and were only given a special dispensation in 1974 because a national fuel crisis (caused by the miners' strike in the winter of 1973/74) meant clubs were not allowed to play under floodlights.

— JOKERS IN THE PACK —

Jeremy Beadle may no longer be about, but the late TV presenter would surely have appreciated these pranks played by Chelsea stars down the years:

- 1970s midfielder Alan Hudson used to come out with the ball at the start of the second half and put it down on the centre spot ready for the Blues to restart the match – even if they had kicked off in the first half. "Huddy did that about ten times a season and usually got away with it," revealed his team-mate, the late Ian Hutchinson. "The odd time we would get caught. That summed up playing for Chelsea – taking the piss and having a laugh."

- Chelsea striker Steve Finnieston celebrated winning promotion from the Second Division in May 1977 by sticking the buttered side of a sandwich on the top of Blues chairman Brian Mears' head. "He took it okay, fortunately," recalled 'Super Jock'.

- 1980s Blues defender Gary Chivers once hid in a laundry basket during a pre-match team talk by Chelsea reserve team manager Tom McInerary. "I was looking out through the holes of the basket and I could see all the other players laughing, but nobody said where I was," explained 'Chiv'. "Then, Tom said, 'Where's that Gary Chivers?' and someone said, 'I think he's out on the pitch doing his warm up', so Tom said, 'Well, tell him to come in!' Somebody went out, came back and said, 'I can't see him.' So Tom went out to have a look himself. At this point I quickly jumped out of the laundry basket, ran into the toilet and then came out of the toilet making out I'd been in there the whole time."

- When Gianfranco Zola arrived at Chelsea from Italian club Parma in 1996 he tried to improve his English by reading thrillers. After ploughing through one book, though, he was baffled by the way it suddenly ended with lots of plotlines unresolved. It was only later that he learned that Blues skipper Dennis Wise had craftily torn out the final chapter!

- A couple of days after Chelsea won the Premier League title for the first time in 2005 a group of Blues players, including skipper John Terry, stormed into the Chelsea TV studios at Stamford Bridge. They then covered presenter Neil Barnett with eggs and flour while he was live on air, before quickly making their escape.

— ALBERT SQUARE BLUES —

The Queen Vic in *EastEnders* may be something of a West Ham pub (no wonder the regulars are all so gloomy!) but, in real life, Albert Square has boasted a fair few Chelsea supporters, including:

Actor	Character
Gemma Bissex	Clare Bates (beauty salon receptionist)
Charlie Brooks	Janine Butcher (scheming daughter of Frank)
Phil Daniels	Kevin Wicks (deceased car salesman)
Michael Greco	Beppe di Marco (nightclub barman)
Michael Higgs	Andy Hunter (gangland bookie)
Martine McCutcheon	Tiffany Raymond (tragic heroine)
Alison Parteger	Sarah Cairns (knife-wielding stalker)
David Spinx	Keith Miller (TV addict layabout)
Daniella Westbrook	Sam Mitchell (original incarnation)

— LONG THROW EXPERTS —

In the late 1930s Chelsea became the first side to use the long throw as a dangerous attacking weapon, thanks to the extraordinary ability of left-half Sam Weaver to hurl the ball deep into the opposition penalty area. According to newspaper reports of the time, some of his throws even reached the far post – a distance few long throw experts have managed since.

Weaver, though, is remembered less often than Ian Hutchinson, who famously created the Blues' winner in the 1970 FA Cup Final replay with a trademark mega-throw into the Leeds penalty box. 'Hutch' was something of a freak of nature, being double-jointed in both shoulders – an accident of birth which allowed him to send the ball soaring through the sky in a whirl of rotating arms. Little wonder, then, that when Chelsea won a throw in the final third of the pitch commentators would often describe it as being "as good as a corner."

— FALLING TO THE WINNERS —

In the following years Chelsea have been knocked out of the FA Cup by the eventual winners of the competition:

Year	Round	Result
1915	Final	Chelsea 0 Sheffield United 3
1920	Semi-final	Chelsea 1 Aston Villa 3
1927	6th round	Cardiff City 3 Chelsea 2*
1930	3rd round	Arsenal 2 Chelsea 0
1932	Semi-final	Chelsea 1 Newcastle United 2
1950	Semi-final	Chelsea 0 Arsenal 1*
1954	3rd round	West Bromwich Albion 1 Chelsea 0
1963	5th round	Manchester United 2 Chelsea 1
1965	Semi-final	Chelsea 0 Liverpool 2

1967	Final	Chelsea 1 Tottenham Hotspur 2
1982	6th round	Chelsea 2 Tottenham Hotspur 3
1986	4th round	Chelsea 1 Liverpool 2
1994	Final	Chelsea 0 Manchester United 4
1996	Semi-final	Chelsea 1 Manchester United 2
1999	6th round	Chelsea 0 Manchester United 2*
2002	Final	Chelsea 0 Arsenal 2
2003	6th round	Chelsea 1 Arsenal 3*
2006	Semi-final	Chelsea 1 Liverpool 2

* Replay

— ROMAN ABRAMOVICH: A POTTED BIOGRAPHY —

- Abramovich was born on 24 October 1966 in Saratov on the Volga River, southern Russia. His mother died of blood poisoning when he just 18 months old and when he was four years old his father was killed in a construction accident. Adopted by his uncle, Abramovich lived for a while in Moscow, then moved to his grandparents' home in the northern region of Komi.
- He studied at the local industrial institute then transferred to Moscow's Gulkin Institute of Oil and Gas, where he sold retread car tyres as a money-spinning sideline.
- After a spell doing national service in the Soviet army, Abramovich concentrated on a business career, trading oil products out of Russia's largest refinery in Ornsk, western Siberia. His entrepreneurial talents were spotted by Boris Berezovsky, Russia's leading tycoon, and together the pair gained a controlling interest in Sibneft, the country's main oil company.
- When Berezovsky went into exile Abramovich became the most important figure at Sibneft. He eventually sold his share in the company to the Russian government-controlled Gazprom for £7.4 billion in 2005.
- In July 2003 Abramovich agreed a deal with then Chelsea chairman Ken Bates to buy his majority shareholding in the club, while also underwriting the significant debts built up by Chelsea Village. He immediately bankrolled a spending spree by then manager Claudio Ranieri to the tune of £100 million.
- Abramovich, who in 2007 divorced his second wife Irina with whom he has five children, enjoys a lifestyle befitting a man who, according to the Sunday Times rich list, is the second wealthiest person in Britain (behind steel magnate Lakshmi Mittal). He has a home in London, a 440-acre site in Sussex, owns three yachts (including the £72 million Pelorus, formerly owned by Saudi billionaire Al Sheik Modhassan) and a private Boeing 737 jet.

— AUSSIE BLUES —

As anyone who has ever glanced at an Australian pools coupon knows there is a Chelsea FC down under. Hailing from Melbourne, and with a largely ex-pat Croatian fanbase the team takes its name from a local suburb and has no connection with the 'real' Chelsea.

— AND YOUR NUMBER NINE THIS WEEK IS . . . —

Since squad numbers were introduced at the start of the 1993/94 season, the number 9 shirt has been worn by more Chelsea players than any other:

Years	Chelsea number 9
1993–94	Tony Cascarino
1994–96	Mark Stein
1996–99	Gianluca Vialli
1999–2000	Chris Sutton
2000–04	Jimmy Floyd Hasselbaink
2004–05	Mateja Kezman
2005–06	Hernan Crespo
2006–07	Khalid Boulahrouz
2007–08	Steve Sidwell
2008–09	Franco di Santo
2011–	Fernando Torres

— TWO-TIME BLUES —

A handful of players have found the lure of Stamford Bridge so irresistible they have returned to Chelsea for a second spell at the club:

Player	Year transferred	Year returned
Bob Whittingham	1914 (to Sth. Shields)	1919 (from Stoke City)
Alec Cheyne	1932 (to Nimes)	1934 (from Nimes)
Ron Greenwood	1945 (to Bradford Park Avenue)	1952 (from Brentford)
Allan Harris	1964 (to Coventry)	1966 (from Coventry)
Charlie Cooke	1972 (to Crystal Palace)	1975 (from Crystal Palace)
Peter Osgood	1974 (to Southampton)	1979 (from Philadelphia Furies)
Alan Hudson	1974 (to Stoke City)	1983 (from Seattle Sounders)
Peter Bonetti	1975 (to St. Louis Stars)	1975 (from St. Louis Stars)

John Hollins	1975 (to QPR)	1983 (from Arsenal)
Steve Wicks	1979 (to Derby)	1986 (from QPR)
Nigel Spackman	1987 (to Liverpool)	1992 (from Glasgow Rangers)
Ken Monkou	1992 (to Southampton)	2002 (out of contract)
Graeme Le Saux	1993 (to Blackburn)	1997 (from Blackburn)

— TEAM OF THE CENTURY —

In 2005, Blues fans were invited to vote for their greatest ever Chelsea team on the club's official website, www.chelseafc.com. 49 different players were nominated but, once the votes were all counted, the team chosen by the supporters and unveiled at a Centenary dinner at Stamford Bridge in August 2005 looked like this:

Peter Bonetti

Steve Clarke   Marcel Desailly   John Terry   Graeme Le Saux

Dennis Wise   Frank Lampard   Charlie Cooke

Gianfranco Zola

Peter Osgood   Bobby Tambling

— NON-SCORING STRIKERS —

Chelsea have made an unfortunate habit of splashing out big money on forwards who subsequently fail to live up to expectations. The prototype misfiring striker was the Blues' first £100,000 signing, Tony Hateley, although his tally of six goals in 27 league games was positively Greaves-like compared to the desperate goals/games and pounds spent ratios of some of his successors.

Heading the list of striking flops is Chris Sutton. Chelsea's first £10 million player endured a miserable season at the Bridge in 1999/2000, notching just one Premiership goal all year. Unsurprisingly, at the end of the campaign he was swiftly sold off to Celtic for a substantial loss.

'Striker'	Transfer fee	Premiership Games*	Goals	Games/ Goals	£/ Goals
Chris Sutton	£10m	28	1	28	£10 m
Fernando Torres	£50m	46	7	6.57	£7.14m
Pierluigi Casiraghi	£5.4m	10	1	10	£5.4m

| Mateja Kezman | £5m | 25 | 4 | 6.25 | £1.25m |
| Robert Fleck | £2.1m | 38 | 3 | 12.66 | £700,000 |

* including substitute appearances

— WHAT A CRACKER! —

Winners of the official Chelsea 'Goal of the Season' award:

Year	Player	Result
2007	Michael Essien	Chelsea 1 Arsenal 1
2008	Juliano Belletti	Chelsea 2 Tottenham 0
2009	Michael Essien	Chelsea 1 Barcelona 1 (Champs Lge)
2010	Ashley Cole	Chelsea 7 Sunderland 2
2011	Ramires	Chelsea 2 Manchester City 0
2012	Ramires	Barcelona 2 Chelsea 2 (Champs Lge)

— 'BEAUTIFUL UNCERTAINTY' —

Chelsea have often been an unpredictable club, superb against-the-odds victories frequently being followed by unexpected defeats against lesser opposition. Even hardened Blues fans, though, must have been surprised when their club followed up an emphatic 8–0 win at Millwall on Boxing Day 1945 with a 7–0 loss at Southampton just three days later.

With the Londoners fielding exactly the same line up in both encounters, the reporter from *The Times* struggled to pinpoint a logical reason for the dramatic swing in the Blues' fortunes. In the end, it appears, he just gave up and put it down to "the beautiful uncertainty of football".

— SPORTING ALL-ROUNDERS —

A handful of Chelsea players have excelled in other sports, and they include:

- England international Max Woosnam (1914) won four 'blues' at Cambridge and went on to play Davis Cup tennis for Great Britain.
- Goalkeeper Benjamin Howard Baker (1921–25) competed in the high jump event at the Olympic Games in 1912 and 1920. A fine tennis player, he also appeared at Wimbledon in the All-England Lawn Tennis championship.

- John Jackson (1933–39) was a Scottish international goalkeeper who later became a professional golfer.
- Clive Walker (1977–84) was a top sprinter as a schoolboy in Oxford, and once recorded a time of 11.2 seconds in a 100m race at Stamford Bridge – not bad, especially as he was wearing football boots!
- Paul Williams (1983) made just one appearance for the Blues, against Oldham in April 1983, and then competed in the London Marathon the following week.
- Nigel Spackman (1983–87 and 1992–96) represented Hampshire at cross-country as a schoolboy.
- Since retiring from football, Roy Wegerle (1986–88) has competed in a number of professional golf tournaments.
- When he was 16, Michael Duberry (1994–98) came second for England in the Home Nations triple jump.
- Bolo Zenden (2001–04) practised judo for 12 years in his native Holland and is a black belt.
- Wayne Bridge (2003–09) represented Hampshire as a sprinter when he was young, recording a best time for the 100m of 11.2 seconds.

— CUP WINNERS' CUP DOUBLE —

Chelsea are the only British club to have won the European Cup Winners' Cup twice. The Blues triumphed against Real Madrid in Athens in 1971 and, again, against Stuttgart in Stockholm in 1998. The other clubs from these shores to win the trophy – Tottenham (1963), West Ham (1965), Manchester City (1970), Glasgow Rangers (1972), Aberdeen (1983), Everton (1985), Manchester United (1991) and Arsenal (1994) – only managed one win each.

— THE £10,000 GOAL —

At the start of the 2005/06 season Chelsea set a new top flight record by going six league games at the start of the season without conceding a single goal. With the Blues threatening to run away with the Premiership, *The Sun* newspaper decided to up the stakes by offering a £10,000 cash prize to the first opposition player to breach Chelsea's watertight defence. In the 43rd minute of the seventh game of the season Aston Villa's Luke Moore claimed the money when he struck the ball past Petr Cech – unfortunately for the young striker, under the terms of *The Sun*'s offer, he had to donate the hefty cheque to charity.

— SHORT, BUT NOT SO SWEET —

Of the more than 50 players who have made just one appearance for Chelsea, a number have endured nightmare matches:

- Goalkeeper Stanley Macintosh conceded six goals in a 6–2 thrashing at Derby on 6 December 1930.
- Rookie keeper Les Fridge fared little better, letting in five on his first and last appearance at home to Watford on 5 May 1986. Chelsea lost the game 5–1. Michael Pinner also conceded five goals in his only appearance for the Blues, a 5–4 home defeat by Wolves on 20 April 1962.
- Centre-half Frank Wolff and right-winger James Toomer played their only games for the Blues in a 7–1 defeat by Crystal Palace in the FA Cup on 18 November 1905. The Chelsea side was essentially a reserve team as a league fixture was scheduled for the same day.
- Former Morton players Billy Sinclair and Jim Smart both made one-off appearances for the Blues at Burnley in a 6–2 defeat on 24 April 1965. Again, Chelsea fielded a severely weakened team as manager Tommy Docherty had sent eight first-team players home for a breach of club discipline during their stay at a Blackpool hotel.
- More recently, Joel Kitamirike's one game for the Blues was the desperately disappointing 2–0 Uefa Cup defeat away to Hapoel Tel Aviv on 1 November 2001. The young defender was called up for the first team after a number of established players, including Marcel Desailly, Emmanuel Petit and Graeme Le Saux, chose not to travel to Israel at a time of local and international tension.

— SCORING STREAKER —

Streakers are nothing new at football matches, but it's unusual for one to actually score a goal. However, that's what happened during the League Cup tie between Liverpool and Chelsea at Anfield on 1 November 2000, when a naked male ran onto the pitch, intercepted a pass from Gianfranco Zola, dribbled through the Blues' defence, and then unleashed a fierce shot past Ed de Goey. The 'goal', of course, was disallowed but Chelsea still lost the match 2–1.

The pitch invader was later named as Mark Roberts, a rather tiresome serial streaker who has revealed all at numerous sporting events, including Wimbledon, the US Super Bowl and the World Snooker Championship final.

— CHELSEA CRICKETERS —

In the past it was quite common for footballers to play professional cricket during the summer. Like most clubs, Chelsea have fielded a number of players who were also handy with bat and ball:

Jimmy Windridge (1905–10) played football for England and cricket for Warwickshire.

Willy 'Fatty' Foulke (1905–06) was Chelsea's first ever goalkeeper and played four times for Derbyshire.

Joe Payne (1938–46) played Minor Counties cricket for Bedfordshire.

Frank Mitchell (1949–52) made 17 first-class appearances for Warwickshire.

Ron Tindall (1955–61) made over 170 appearances for Surrey.

Ron Harris (1962–80) was a batsman/wicketkeeper on the groundstaff at Lord's but turned down the chance to become a cricketer, choosing to sign for Chelsea instead.

Geoff Hurst (manager 1979–81) made a handful of appearances for Essex.

— NOW, WHICH WAY ARE WE KICKING, AGAIN? —

In a bizarre match played at Stamford Bridge between Chelsea and Swindon Town on 11 February 1989 three of the five goals scored were own goals. Swindon's Jonathan Gittens and Ross MacLaren helpfully netted for the Blues, while Joe McLaughlin got on the scoresheet for the visitors. Chelsea won the match 3–2, with all the goals coming in the first half.

— CHELSEA ACROSS THE POND —

Chelsea is a popular name for towns, villages and districts in the United States. Here are six of them:

Chelsea, Alabama (population, 2,949)
Chelsea, Maine (pop, 2,559)
Chelsea, Massachusetts (pop, 35,177)
Chelsea, Michigan (pop, 4,398)
Chelsea, Oklahoma (pop, 2,136)
Chelsea, Vermont (pop, 1,250)

— A SHED-LOAD OF SMITHS —

Seven men called Smith have played for Chelsea, making this the most common surname among Blues players in the club's history.

- Philip Smith made just one appearance for the Blues, in a 1–0 defeat away to Bristol city on 16 April 1910.
- Full-back George Smith made 370 appearances for the club between 1921 and 1930.
- Half-back Stephen Smith made his debut two days after George in 1921, but only went on to make a total of 23 appearances for the Blues.

- Welsh full-back Jack Smith made his debut in 1938, but his Chelsea career was cut short by the outbreak of World War II.
- Striker Bobby Smith scored 30 goals for Chelsea in 86 games in the 1950s and went on to figure in Tottenham's 1961 Double-winning team.
- Left-winger Jimmy Smith was a bit-part player on the Bridge scene during the early 1950s.
- Youth product Jimmy Smith made his debut as a sub against Newcastle in the final match of the 2005/06 season.

— SIGNING OFF IN STYLE —

A team of Chelsea players who won a cup-winners' medal in their last game for the club:

1. Frode Grodas (FA Cup, 1997)
2. Danny Granville (European Cup Winners' Cup, 1998)
3. Scott Minto (FA Cup, 1997)
4. Juliano Belletti (FA Cup, 2010)
5. Frank Sinclair (League Cup, 1998)
6. Steve Clarke (European Cup Winners' Cup, 1998)
7. Didier Deschamps (FA Cup, 2000)
8. Michael Ballack (FA Cup, 2010)
9. George Weah (FA Cup, 2000)
10. Joe Cole (FA Cup, 2010)
11. Arjen Robben (FA Cup, 2007)
Manager: Guus Hiddink (FA Cup, 2009)

* Unused substitute

— £264 PER SECOND —

Signed on a Bosman free transfer from Barcelona shortly before Gianluca Vialli's dismissal as Chelsea manager, Dutch defender Winston Bogarde endured a miserable four years at Stamford Bridge, making just four starts for the club. To make matters worse, all four games Bogarde began ended in defeat for the Blues:

Date	Result
17 September 2000	Chelsea 0 Leicester City 2
28 September 2000	St Gallen 2 Chelsea 0
1 November 2000	Liverpool 2 Chelsea 1
25 November 2000	Everton 2 Chelsea 1

Yet there were compensations – notably in the form of a salary package estimated to be in the region of £2 million per year. If this figure is correct, Bogarde was paid at a rate of £15,841 for every minute or £264 per second he appeared on the pitch for the Chelsea first team. Nice work if you can get it!

— CHELSEA BEST NICKNAMES XI —

1. The Cat (Peter Bonetti)
2. Chopper (Ron Harris)
3. Jamaica (Paul Elliott)
4. Butch (Ray Wilkins)
5. The Rock (Marcel Desailly)
6. The Wall (Emerson Thome)
7. The Rabbit (Eric Parsons)
8. The Sponge (Tommy Baldwin)
9. The Wig (Kerry Dixon)
10. Jukebox (Gordon Durie)
11. The Rat (Dennis Wise)

Manager: The Doc (Tommy Docherty)

— GREEN (OR WHITE!) IS THE COLOUR —

The song *Blue is the Colour* has been a feature of matchdays at Stamford Bridge since it was first recorded by the Chelsea squad in 1972. Variations of the song can also be heard at the stadiums of the following clubs:

- **HJK Helsinki:** The club's first team squad recorded a version of *Blue is the Colour* in 1973. The song, whose Finnish title translates into English as 'Again Terraces are Filled', is still played before HJK home games.
- **Vancouver Whitecaps:** The Canadian soccer team re-recorded the song as *White is the Colour* in 1978 and it became a local hit. In 2002 the Scottish rock duo The Proclaimers recorded their own version of *White is the Colour* while on tour in Vancouver, performing the song live during the half-time interval of a Whitecaps match.
- **Saskatchewan Roughriders:** The Canadian Football League outfit are another team to have adapted the original song lyrics, recording a version entitled *Green is the Colour*.
- **Various Czech teams:** In 1973 Czech singer Frantilek 'Ringo' Lech recorded a song called *Green is the Grass* based on *Blue is the Colour*. Lech's song became a popular football anthem in the former Czechoslovakia.

— POINTLESS QUESTION —

In the popular BBC1 quiz show *Pointless* contestants are asked questions based on the answers given by 100 people in 100 seconds, the idea being to find the most obscure correct answer in any particular category. A 2011 edition of the programme saw the two teams of finalists asked to name a Chelsea manager who had worked under Roman Abramovich before the arrival of Andre Villas-Boas. Surprisingly, all six Blues bosses on the list – even the charismatic Jose Mourinho – recorded extremely low scores, suggesting that the frequent comings and goings in the Chelsea manager's office had left the general public somewhat baffled and bemused:

Manager	Points (out of 100)
Jose Mourinho	19
Carlo Ancelotti	16
Avram Grant	11
Guus Hiddink	10
Claudio Ranieri	9
Luiz Felipe Scolari	5

Looking at these pitiful scores, one can only imagine that a typical response to the question "Name as many of the six Chelsea managers under Roman Abramovich . . ." went something like this:

"Ah yes, the first one was that Italian, 'The Tinkerman' they called him, but what was his name? Can't remember. Then it was, you know, the Portuguese bloke with the silver-grey hair and the expensive coat. Won a lot of trophies at Chelsea, thought he was the bees' knees, a bit cocky . . . but his name's slipped my mind. Then it was that gloomy Israeli, looked like he'd just lost a tenner. Sorry, got a blank on him, too. After that, wasn't there that Gene Hackman-lookalike who couldn't speak English very well? He didn't last long, not long enough for him to register and, er, then there was another one who didn't stay long – Belgian wasn't he, or Dutch? Blimey, I'm not doing very well here, am I? But I do know the most recent one, another Italian, Carlos something . . . now, what's his surname? Sorry, can't remember that either . . ."

In another edition of *Pointless*, meanwhile, the 100-strong focus group was asked to name the clubs which played at a dozen Premier League grounds. The top four correct responses were:

Ground	Club	Points (out of 100)
Old Trafford	Manchester United	74
Anfield	Liverpool	60

| The Emirates | Arsenal | 51 |
| Stamford Bridge | Chelsea | 50 |

Again, the fact that 50 people out of 100 don't know that Chelsea play at Stamford Bridge is rather perplexing. Don't they teach kids anything in school these days?

— CHELSEA HOST BRIDGE PARTIES —

Apart from Chelsea's victories in 1955, 2005 and 2006, Stamford Bridge has been the venue for league title celebrations on three other occasions. Unfortunately, those enjoying the party were the players and fans of the opposition:

- On 22 April 1933 Arsenal clinched the title at the Bridge with a 3–1 victory in front of a huge crowd of 72,260.
- The following year the Gunners returned to SW6 with the title in their sights. This time a 2–2 draw was sufficient to get the Gunners' champagne corks popping.
- On 3 May 1986 Liverpool pipped local rivals Everton for the title after a single goal by Kenny Dalglish gave the Reds victory over Chelsea at Stamford Bridge.

— FIRST DAY HIGHS AND LOWS —

- Chelsea's best start to a season came way back in 1906 when the Blues thrashed Glossop North End 9–2 in a Second Division fixture at Stamford Bridge on the opening day. Striker George 'Gatling Gun' Hilsdon, who was making his Chelsea debut having been recently been signed from West Ham, scored five of the goals.
- The Blues recorded their biggest top-flight opening day victory in 2010, thrashing newly-promoted West Bromwich Albion 6–0 at the Bridge. With three goals, centre-forward Didier Drogba was the star of the show. As if to prove the result was no fluke, Chelsea hammered Wigan by precisely the same score the following week.
- The Blues' worst opening day defeat came in 1958 when they crashed 5–2 at Manchester United, Bobby Charlton scoring a hat-trick for the home side.
- Chelsea's most humiliating start to a season, though, was in 1974 when the Blues lost 2–0 to newly-promoted Carlisle United at Stamford Bridge in the Cumbrians' first-ever match in the top flight (and the first match in front of the new East Stand). It was a taste of things to come for the Londoners, who were relegated at the end of the season along with Carlisle and Luton.

— LEAGUE CUP BOYCOTT —

In the early years of the League Cup the competition was seen by many big clubs as an unwanted addition to an already crowded fixture list. Chelsea were among those to boycott the competition, failing to enter a team in the following seasons: 1961/62, 1962/63 and 1965/66.

In the last of these three seasons Chelsea were the holders of the League Cup trophy but still decided against defending their title. This decision was taken because the club had qualified for the Fairs Cup (the precursor of the UEFA Cup) and it was felt that competing in the League Cup as well would cause difficulties with fixture congestion.

— BLUE LIBRARY —

Chelsea players and managers to have published autobiographies include:

Carlo Ancelotti: *The Beautiful Games of an Ordinary Genius: My Autobiography* (2010)
Roy Bentley: *Going For Goal* (1955) and *Roy Wonder* (2005)
Alan Birchenall: *Bring Back The Birch* (2000)
Peter Bonetti: *Leaping To Fame* (1968)
Paul Canoville: *Black and Blue* (2008)
Tony Cascarino: *Full Time* (2000)
Ashley Cole: *My Defence* (2006)
Joe Cole: *My Autobiography* (2010)
Charlie Cooke: *The Bonnie Prince* (2006)
Kerry Dixon: *Kerry* (1986)
Tommy Docherty: *The Doc* (2006)
Didier Drogba: *The Autobiography* (2008)
Jimmy Greaves: *Greavsie* (2003)
Ruud Gullit: *My Autobiography* (1998)
Ron Harris: *Soccer The Hard Way* (1970) and *Chopper: A Chelsea Legend* (2004)
Alan Hudson: *The Working Man's Ballet* (1998)
Joey Jones: *Oh Joey, Joey!* (2005)
Vinnie Jones: *Vinnie* (1998)
Frank Lampard: *Totally Frank* (2006)
Graeme Le Saux: *Left Field* (2007)
Peter Osgood: *Ossie The Wizard* (1969) and *Ossie: King of Stamford Bridge* (2002)
Mickey Thomas: *Kickups, Hiccups, Lockups: The Autobiography* (2008)
Terry Venables: *Venables* (1994)
Dennis Wise: *The Autobiography* (1999)

— JOKER GILES UPSETS TOFFEES —

Following Chelsea's victory over Everton in the first leg of the Carling Cup semi-final at Stamford Bridge in January 2008, columnist Giles Smith wrote an article on the club's official website jokingly suggesting that the rules of the competition should be changed to allow the defeated side to pull out of the tie after the first match. It would be useful, he wrote, "if a team trailing after the first leg were given the choice whether to proceed with the second leg or whether to call it a day after 90 minutes, leaving the other side to go through. Bingo, no more tiresome second leg formalities."

With Chelsea having seen off Everton despite being reduced to ten men by the sending off of John Mikel Obi, Smith wondered whether the Toffees might not prefer to throw in the towel rather than risk further humiliation in the return leg. This comment, although clearly delivered with tongue firmly in cheek, caused a storm of outrage on Merseyside with *The Liverpool Echo* suggesting that the article "effortlessly encapsulated the arrogant, smug nature of Chelsea supporters." Everton FC duly sent an official complaint, while the Chelsea website was inundated with angry emails from offended Toffees fans. Sadly for them, Smith's madcap idea looked altogether less daft after Chelsea won the second leg as well.

— 1907: A FIRST PROMOTION —

In only their second year as a Football League club Chelsea gained promotion to the First Division along with champions Nottingham Forest. For the final match of the season at home to Gainsborough Trinity, the Chelsea programme celebrated this achievement, with the following words:

"There is no necessity for us to perform a solo on the Chelsea trumpet. That tune has been played with orchestral effects by the full band of the public press and our legion of followers. That the Chelsea team has accomplished a wonderful feat in gaining promotion, in the second year of the club's existence, to the Premier League is beyond cavil."

Top Six 1906/07

	P	W	D	L	F	A	Pts
Nottingham Forest	38	28	4	6	74	36	60
Chelsea	38	26	5	7	80	34	57
Leicester City	38	20	8	10	62	39	48
West Bromwich Albion	38	21	5	12	83	45	47
Bradford City	38	21	5	12	70	53	47
Wolverhampton Wanderers	38	17	7	14	66	53	41

— CHELSEA KIT SPONSORS —

Starting with Gulf Air during the promotion season of 1983/84, ten companies have sponsored Chelsea's shirts:

Gulf Air (second half of 1983/84 season)
Bai Lin Tea (selected matches during1986/87)
Grange Farm (selected matches during1986/87)
Simod (selected matches during1986/87)
Commodore (1987–93)
Amiga (1993/94)
Coors (1994–97)
Autoglass (1997–2001)
Emirates (2001–2005)
Samsung (2005–)

— GARY'S OUR BETE NOIRE —

Gary Bannister may not be one of the most lauded footballers of the domestic game – the journeyman striker never won an England cap and spent all of his career with fairly unfashionable clubs – but, make no mistake, the very mention of his name is probably enough to send shivers down the spine of Chelsea defenders of the 1980s and early 1990s. Why? Well, Bannister had the unhappy knack of scoring against the Blues, and it didn't seem much to matter whether he was the wearing the blue-and-white stripes of Sheffield Wednesday, the hoops of QPR or the red jersey of Nottingham Forest – if Gazza was lining up against the famous blue shirts, he invariably got on the scoresheet. In fact, his total of 14 goals in matches against Chelsea is a record by an opposition player – just beating Alan Shearer, but well ahead of other legendary strikers like Gary Lineker, Ian Rush and Thierry Henry. If Bannister was still playing it might be tempting fate to mention his impressive feat, but bearing in mind that he hung his boots up more than 15 years ago and is no longer a threat to the Blues rearguard, it seems only right to acknowledge his scoring exploits and list the games in which he broke Chelsea hearts:

Date	Result	Bannister Goals
5 Dec 1981	Chelsea 2 Sheffield Weds 1	1
25 Sept 1982	Sheffield Weds 3 Chelsea 2	1
2 May 1983	Chelsea 1 Sheffield Weds 1	1
21 Jan 1984	Chelsea 3 Sheffield Weds 2	1
26 Dec 1984	QPR 2 Chelsea 2	1
31 March 1986	QPR 6 Chelsea 0	3
18 April 1987	QPR 1 Chelsea 1	1

| 12 Sept 1987 | QPR 3 Chelsea 1 | 3 |
| 16 Jan 1993 | Nottingham Forest 3 Chelsea 0 | 2 |

Yes, Gary, we particularly like the way you disappeared off the scoring scene for six years and then popped up again to bang in two goals against the Blues in 1993 . . . not!

— FAN POWER —

Fans often complain that their opinions are ignored, but on a number of occasions when Chelsea supporters have made their feelings clear the powers-that-be have taken note:

- August 1971: Shed idol Peter Osgood was put on the transfer list by Chelsea boss Dave Sexton for "lack of effort". Fans demonstrated outside the Bridge with placards reading 'Don't go, Ossie!' and 'Sexton must relent'. Sexton did relent and took Osgood off the list.
- May 1981: After watching their side fail to score in the last nine matches of the season, 2,000 Chelsea fans invaded the Stamford Bridge pitch on the final day of the campaign calling for chairman Brian Mears to resign. Having initially stated that he had no intention of standing down, Mears eventually quit on 2 June 1981.
- May 1996: Following Glenn Hoddle's appointment as England coach, press reports suggested that former Arsenal manager George Graham was the favourite to succeed him at Stamford Bridge. The fans, though, were adamant that they didn't want the defensive-minded Graham and instead hailed star player Ruud Gullit as their preferred choice in the final home game of the season. A few days later Gullit was appointed player/manager of the Blues.
- 2003/04 season: While media speculation linked England coach Sven Goran Eriksson with the Chelsea job, supporters made it clear that the bespectacled, bed-hopping Swede was not wanted at Stamford Bridge. Chants of 'We don't need Eriksson' rang out at several matches and the Chelsea hierarchy eventually settled on Jose Mourinho as a replacement for Claudio Ranieri.

— SEXY FAVES —

During the 2000/01 season the matchday Chelsea programme asked the players to nominate the three sexiest people in the world. The most popular nominations were:

Jennifer Lopez
Cameron Diaz
Jennifer Aniston
Kelly Brooke

The only male to be nominated was Brad Pitt (one of the three choices of
Roberto di Matteo).

— GREAVSIE'S EIGHT-GOAL SALVO —

In season 1959/60 Jimmy Greaves notched an incredible total of eight goals
in two First Division games against the same team, Preston North End. The
Lancashire side visited Stamford Bridge on the opening day of the campaign
and came away with a point from an entertaining 4–4 draw, Greaves scoring
three of the Blues' goals. In the return fixture a week before Christmas,
Jimmy did even better, claiming all five of Chelsea's goals in a dramatic 5–4
win at Deepdale.

Greaves' eight-goal haul against the Lilywhites established a new
Chelsea record, surpassing the seven goals George Hilsdon managed in
total against Glossop North End in 1906/07.

Peter Osgood also hit eight goals in two European Cup Winners Cup
matches against Luxembourg minnows Jeunesse Hautcharage in September
1971. Ossie grabbed a hat-trick in the Blues' 8–0 away leg victory and followed
that up with five goals in Chelsea's record 13–0 win at the Bridge in the return.

— ONE TEAM IN LONDON —

Random facts from the Blues' long history of encounters with other teams
from the capital:

- Chelsea's first-ever London derby was against Southern United, a
  non-league outfit from Nunhead, in the second preliminary round
  of the FA Cup on 28 October 1905. Despite having to play a defender
  in goal for the whole 90 minutes, the Blues came away from south
  London with a 1–0 win.
- The Blues' biggest-ever win in a London derby was a 7–1 thrashing
  of Millwall in a League Cup first round tie at The Den in 1960. The
  west Londoners also managed seven goals against Orient in 1979,
  winning a Second Division fixture at Brisbane Road 7–3.
- In the Premier League era, the Blues recorded their biggest derby
  win against Tottenham in 1997, smashing the north Londoners 6–1
  at White Hart Lane thanks in part to a hat-trick by lanky Norwegian
  striker Tore Andre Flo. Blues also beat QPR 6–1 at home in 2012.

- The Blues suffered their worst-ever defeat in a derby in 1986, crashing 6–0 on the plastic pitch at QPR in a First Division fixture.
- Chelsea first finished as London's highest-placed club in 1913/14. In all, the Blues have been the capital's top club on 14 occasions, most recently in 2010/11.
- The Blues have played more league games against north London rivals Arsenal than any other club. Since first meeting in 1907 – a 2–1 win for the west Londoners in front of a 55,000 crowd at Stamford Bridge – the two clubs have clashed 150 times, the Gunners leading the way with 61 victories to the Blues' 44.
- The Blues enjoyed their best ever run in London derbies against Tottenham between 1990 and 2006, remaining undefeated in 32 top-flight matches (21 wins, 11 draws).
- No player has appeared in more London derbies during the Premier League era than Frank Lampard. The Blues midfielder has turned out 126 times against opponents from the capital, including 38 derbies with his first club, West Ham.

— SCANDAL SITES —

Over the years Chelsea stars have been involved in numerous bust ups with the management, run-ins with the police and various other assorted scandalous episodes. Some of the most infamous incidents took place at the following locations:

- Blackpool, April 1965: Manager Tommy Docherty sent home eight players, including Terry Venables, George Graham and John Hollins, when they disobeyed his instruction to stay in the team hotel and instead went out drinking on the Golden Mile.
- Old Street Police Station, 1968: Tommy Baldwin was charged with assault after throwing a vodka bottle out of a speeding car and then being involved in a scuffle with police at the station. Baldwin was sentenced to four months in prison, although following an appeal the sentence was suspended.
- Barbarella's restaurant, Fulham Road, January 1969: Peter Osgood, John Boyle and Charlie Cooke spent a drunken afternoon here when they should have been receiving treatment at the Bridge for minor injuries. Manager Dave Sexton was not amused and dropped the trio for the Blues' next match at Southampton – which Chelsea lost 5–0.
- King's Road, January 1972: Peter Osgood was arrested by the police and charged with being drunk and disorderly after singing 'We're on our way to Wembley!' following Chelsea's epic League Cup

semi-final defeat of Tottenham. The case against Osgood was dismissed by the magistrate the next day.

- Scribes West nightclub, Kensington, October 1994: After hailing a taxi outside the club owned by then England manager Terry Venables, Dennis Wise became involved in a fracas with the driver. Wise was arrested and charged with criminal damage and assault. Initially found guilty and sentenced to three months in prison, his conviction was overturned on appeal.

- Posthouse Hotel, Heathrow, September 2001: Four Chelsea players – Frank Lampard, John Terry, Eidur Gudjohnsen and Jody Morris – were each fined two weeks' wages after their drunken antics in the hotel bar offended American tourists waiting for flights home following the Al-Qaida attacks on the US on September 11th.

- The Wellington Club, Knightsbridge, January 2002: John Terry and Jody Morris were involved in an incident with a bouncer at the club which led to them appearing at Middlesex Guildhall Crown Court in August 2002. Terry was charged with a number of offences, including wounding with intent to cause grievous bodily harm, while Morris was charged with affray. The jury found both players not guilty on all counts.

- B&Q store, Dartford, January 2007: While on loan at Portsmouth Blues defender Glen Johnson was spotted putting a toilet seat into a box with a lower price tag by a 74-year-old security guard. Along with Millwall striker Ben May, he also hid a set of taps under a sink to avoid paying for them. Police were called to the scene and the pair were handed on-the-spot fines of £80 each.

— KEN'S DOUBLE NATIONALITY —

Ken Armstrong, a key member of the Blues' 1955 championship-winning team, is the only Chelsea player to have won international caps for two countries. In 1955 Armstrong played his only game for England, in the 7–2 thrashing of Scotland at Wembley. In 1957, after setting a then Chelsea appearance record of 402 matches, he emigrated to New Zealand and, the following year, made the first of 13 international appearances for the Kiwis.

— FOREIGN LEGION STALWARTS —

Sixteen overseas players have made more than 200 appearances for Chelsea and they are:

Petr Cech (2004–)	369 apps
Didier Drogba (2004–)	341 apps

Gianfranco Zola (1996–2003)	312 apps
Eidur Gudjohnsen (2000–06)	263 apps
Salomon Kalou (2006–)	254 apps
Michael Essien (2005–)	247 apps
John Mikel Obi (2006–)	239 apps
Florent Malouda (2007–)	229 apps
William Gallas (2001–06)	225 apps
Marcel Desailly (1998–2004)	222 apps
Claude Makelele (2003–08)	217 apps
Carlo Cudicini (1999–2009)	216 apps
Paulo Ferreira (2004–)	210 apps
Ricardo Carvalho (2004–10)	210 apps
Dan Petrescu (1995–2000)	208 apps
Frank Leboeuf (1996–2001)	204 apps

— POPPY ON THEIR CHESTS —

The matches when the Chelsea team have worn a poppy on their shirts to mark Remembrance Day:

Date	Result
8 Nov 2009	Chelsea 1 Manchester United 0
14 Nov 2010	Chelsea 0 Sunderland 3
29 Oct 2011	Chelsea 3 Arsenal 5

— A TRIO OF GOALKEEPERS —

In a strange game at Reading on 14 October 2006 Chelsea were forced to use no fewer than three goalkeepers. The original selection between the posts, Petr Cech, didn't last long as he was carried off after a first-minute challenge by Stephen Hunt left him with a fractured skull. Carlo Cudicini took his place, but near the end of the match was also whisked off to hospital following a clash with Reading defender Ibrahima Sonko. Skipper John Terry took over between the sticks and, in the remaining two minutes, was able to preserve Chelsea's clean sheet in a hard-fought 1–0 win.

— FLIRTATION WITH DISASTER —

In season 1982/83 Chelsea only narrowly avoided relegation to the old Third Division. Eventually, thanks to a 1–0 win at Bolton and a 0–0 draw at home to Middlesbrough in their last two games, the Blues finished two places above the drop zone. Nonetheless, Chelsea's final position of 18th in the old Second Division remains the club's lowest ever league placing.

At the end of a season to forget for Blues fans the bottom six of the Second Division looked like this:

		P	W	D	L	F	A	Pts
17	Charlton Athletic	42	13	9	20	63	84	48
18	Chelsea	42	11	14	17	51	61	47
19	Grimsby Town	42	12	11	19	45	70	47
20	Rotherham United	42	10	15	17	45	68	45
21	Burnley	42	12	8	22	56	66	44
22	Bolton Wanderers	42	11	11	20	42	61	44

— LEADING SCORERS IN ALL COMPETITIONS —

League: Bobby Tambling, 164 goals
FA Cup: Bobby Tambling, 25 goals
League Cup: Kerry Dixon, 25 goals
Premier League: Frank Lampard, 126 goals
Europe: Didier Drogba, 34 goals

— FA PREMIER LEAGUE PLAYER OF THE MONTH —

Inaugurated at the start of the 1994/95 season, this award has been won 14 times by Chelsea players:

Month	Player
December 1996	Gianfranco Zola
October 2002	Gianfranco Zola
September 2003	Frank Lampard
November 2004	Arjen Robben
January 2005	John Terry
March 2005	Joe Cole
April 2005	Didier Drogba
October 2005	Frank Lampard
March 2007	Petr Cech
August 2008	Deco
October 2008	Frank Lampard
November 2008	Nicolas Anelka
March 2010	Florent Malouda
March 2011	David Luiz

— CALLING NUMBER 52 —

When Jacob Mellis made his Chelsea debut as a substitute at home to MSK Zilina in the Champions League on 23 November 2010 he did so in the highest shirt number ever worn by a Blues player, 52.

— THE POETRY OF FOOTBALL —

Peter Osgood's headed equaliser for Chelsea in the 1970 FA Cup Final replay against Leeds at Old Trafford is one of the most famous goals in the history of the club. It was also one of the most spectacular, perhaps best described by this piece of lyrical writing by Geoffrey Green in his match report for *The Times*:

> *"With 10 minutes left they suddenly were level. Theirs, too, was a beautiful goal: more complicated, more finely ingrained, more liquid and created virtually out of nothing. Here was the poetry of football and it came with a magical exchange of passes between Hollins, Hutchinson, Osgood and then the hard-running Cooke. Over came Cooke's perfect chip and there was Osgood infiltrating from the left blind side to head a magnificent goal."*

— ALLITERATIVE CHELSEA XI —

1. Steve Sherwood (1972–75)
2. Joey Jones (1982–85)
3. Paul Parker (1997)
4. Brian Bason (1972–76)
5. William Williams (1927)
6. George Graham (1964–66)
7. Damien Duff (2003–2006)
8. Didier Deschamps (1999–2000)
9. Didier Drogba (2004–)
10. Barry Bridges (1959–66)
11. Charlie Cooke (1966–78)
Manager: Billy Birrell (1939–52)

— EDDIE'S £50 GOAL —

Midfielder Eddie Newton only scored one goal for Chelsea during the 1996/97 season, but he couldn't have chosen a bigger game in which to find the net – the 1997 FA Cup Final against Middlesbrough. Not only did the goal wrap up a 2–0 victory for the Blues, it also saved him £50 in a 'season's goals' bet with team-mate Frank Sinclair. In the event, both players finished the season on one goal each, so neither player won the money. "I was expecting to take £50 off him after the game," complained Sinclair afterwards, "and the geezer's come up and scored in the FA Cup Final. He's so stingy he had to score."

— HERO AND VILLAIN —

Bustling striker Bobby Smith set an unusual first in the 1955/56 season when he scored for Chelsea in a 2–0 win over Spurs at the Bridge on 15 October 1955 and then, after moving to Tottenham two months later, was on target for the north Londoners against the Blues in the return fixture at White Hart Lane on 25 February 1956 – a game Spurs won 4–0.

A decade later lanky striker Tony Hateley matched Smith's feat, albeit in reverse. First, on 17 September 1966, he scored for Aston Villa in the Blues' famous 6–2 win at Villa Park when Bobby Tambling notched five goals. A month later he signed for Chelsea in a £100,000 deal, and when his old club visited the Bridge on 21 January 1967 he reminded them what they were missing by netting one of the Blues' three goals in a 3–1 win.

— GOALS, GOALS AND MORE GOALS —

The campaigns when Chelsea found the back of the net most times are:

Season	Matches played	Total goals	Leading scorer
1964/65	55	121	Barry Bridges, 27
1960/61	47	117	Jimmy Greaves, 43
2006/07	64	117	Didier Drogba, 33
2009/10	56	142	Didier Drogba, 37

— OLD TRAFFORD FINALS —

The FA Cup Final has only been played twice at Old Trafford, in 1915 and 1970, and on both occasions Chelsea appeared in the final. The 1915 final between the Blues and Sheffield United should have been played at Crystal Palace but was switched to Manchester to make attendance more difficult for London-based fans, so limiting absenteeism by workers carrying out essential war work during World War I.

In 1970 the FA Cup Final replay was played at Old Trafford after the Wembley pitch had been judged too poor to stage a second match. The problem stemmed from a misguided decision by the stadium authorities to allow the Horse of the Year Show to be held at the Twin Towers venue.

— PREMIER LEAGUE BOGEYMEN —

Since the Premiership began in 1992 only four opposition strikers have managed to score a hat-trick against the Blues. The dastardly quartet are:

Year	Player	Result
1997	Dion Dublin	Coventry City 3 Chelsea 2
1997	Patrik Berger	Liverpool 4 Chelsea 2
1999	Kanu	Chelsea 2 Arsenal 3
2011	Robin van Persie	Chelsea 3 Arsenal 5

— CHELSEA SIGNINGS PROMPT TRANSFER DEADLINE —

In a desperate bid to avoid relegation Chelsea splashed out the then sizeable sum of £3,300 on three new players in April 1910. Marshall McEwan, English McConnell and Bob Whittingham all appeared in the final encounter of the season away to fellow strugglers Tottenham which Spurs won 2–1.

Although the signings had not, ultimately, altered Chelsea's fate, the Football League decided that similar panic buys would not be allowed in the future and promptly introduced the transfer deadline.

— KIT DISASTERS —

Chelsea's royal blue home kit has long been considered as one of the most stylish in the league. The Blues, though, have committed a few fashion blunders over the years and, on occasions, have even been reduced to borrowing their opponents' kit!

- In a fifth round FA Cup replay against Chesterfield in 1950, Chelsea wore Fulham shirts complete with their neighbours' crest. This odd episode stemmed from the FA's insistence that, in the event of a kit clash, both teams should change colours. Unfortunately, the second choice kits also clashed so, following a toss of the coin, Chelsea were forced to look elsewhere and, lacking a third-choice kit, had to make do with a loan from the Cottagers.
- In the 1966 FA Cup semi-final against Sheffield Wednesday at Villa Park Chelsea wore a blue-and-black striped kit based on Inter Milan's colours. The Blues lost the match 2–0 and never wore the kit again.
- In 1973 Chelsea boss Dave Sexton introduced a striking new away kit for the Blues: red shirts, white shorts and green socks. The colours matched those worn by the Hungarian side of 1953 which famously thrashed England 6–3 at Wembley. Sadly, the Magyars' magic failed

to rub off on the Blues, who won just eight away league games in the two seasons they wore the kit.

• Between 1994 and 1996 Chelsea wore an orange and grey away strip which many fans consider their worst ever. Star player Ruud Gullit, who once said he only decided to join the Blues because of their stylish white socks, must have been appalled by this fashion faux pas.

• On 9 April 1997 Chelsea were all set to play Coventry at Highfield Road when the referee decided that the Blues' first-choice blue kit clashed with the home team's sky blue outfit. Having failed to pack their second-choice yellow kit, Chelsea were forced to wear Coventry's red-and-black 'chessboard' away shirts, complete with Peugeot sponsorship logo. After a 15-minute delay while the Chelsea players changed, Coventry (home) beat Coventry (away) 3–1.

— TV NICKNAMES —

A number of Chelsea players have had nicknames derived from popular TV characters. These include:

John Hollins: Ena (after the *Coronation Street* gossip, Ena Sharples)
Eddie McCreadie: Clarence (after the squint-eyed lion in *Daktari*)
John Boyle: Trampas (a character in the 60s Western series, *The Virginian*)
Garry Stanley: Starsky (the character played by Stanley-lookalike Paul Michael Glazer in *Starsky and Hutch*)
David Lee: Rodders (after Rodney Trotter, the Nicholas Lyndhurst character in *Only Fools and Horses*)
Graeme Le Saux: Bergerac, usually shortened to 'Berge' (like Le Saux the TV detective was from the Channel Islands)

— CAPITAL CONNECTIONS —

Chelsea have the second-best record in London derbies since the Premier League was founded in 1992. Arsenal lead the way in this unofficial league table, but the Blues have the Gunners firmly in their sights:

	PL seasons	P	W	D	L	F	A	Pts
Arsenal	20	188	97	53	38	316	178	344
Chelsea	20	188	94	53	41	312	184	335
Tottenham	20	188	58	61	69	244	257	235
West Ham	16	152	46	37	69	150	229	175
Wimbledon	8	80	27	20	33	97	114	101

Fulham	11	100	20	31	49	100	156	91
Charlton	8	78	23	17	38	92	129	86
QPR	5	50	15	15	20	53	63	60
Crystal Palace	4	42	9	12	21	37	74	39
Watford	2	22	2	7	13	17	41	13

— PROGRAMME FACTS —

- The first Chelsea programme, entitled 'The Chelsea FC Chronicle', was published for a friendly match against Liverpool at Stamford Bridge on 4 September 1905. The opening words read: "They're off, Chelsea's opening home match was a friendly pipe-opener against Liverpool at Stamford Bridge. One of the linesmen was none other than J.J. Bentley Esquire, President of the Football League!"
- On 25 December 1948 for the visit of Portsmouth Chelsea became the first club to issue a 16-page magazine-style programme. It cost six old pence (2.5p).
- The ever-expanding page numbers were increased to 20 in 1975, 24 in 1978, 32 in 1985, 40 in 1990, 56 in 1994, 64 in 1997, 68 in 1999 and 74 in 2005. The larger-size page format was first introduced in 1974, although the programme reverted to a smaller, pocket-size format between 1980 and 1983.
- Editors of the programme since 1948 are: Albert Sewell (1948–80), Hugh Hastings (1980–86), Colin Benson (1986–89), Dennis Signey OBE (1989–91), Hayters news agency (1991–94), Neil Barnett (1994–2004), Andrew Winter (2004), Chris Deary (acting editor, 2004), Lee Berry (2004–08) and David Antill (2008–).
- In the 1972/73 season Chelsea's 26 home matches in all competitions were watched by a total of 780,934 spectators who bought 770,932 programmes. This represented an average programme sale over the season of 99%, which is believed to be a world record for any club.
- When Chelsea played away to Jeunesse Hautcharage in the European Cup Winners' Cup in 1971 the Luxembourg side produced a 160-page programme, the longest ever for a Blues match.
- The manager's programme column was introduced as a regular feature at the start of the 1980/81 season when Geoff Hurst was the Blues' boss.
- The captain's column didn't appear until the 1984/85 season when Colin Pates was the skipper.

— JOSE AND HIS AMAZING TECHNICOLOUR OVERCOAT —

In his first season at Stamford Bridge Jose Mourinho was rarely out of the headlines. Such was the obsession with the Chelsea manager that even his clothes, especially a smart grey winter Armani overcoat, provoked much press comment. "He combines the suaveness of Cary Grant with Iberian swagger and a touch of blokeish nonchalence," suggested Rory Ross in *The Daily Telegraph*, one of many journalists to deconstruct Mourinho's personal style. Opposition fans, too, had their say, cheekily claiming in one chant that Mourinho had bought his coat from Matalan.

The coat was also the inspiration for a minor hit single, *Jose And His Amazing Technicolour Overcoat*, by professional impersonator Mario Rosenstock. Based on the song *Any Dream Will Do* from the musical *Joseph and the Technicolour Dreamcoat*, the tongue-in-cheek record reached number 45 in the charts in March 2006. By then, however, Jose's coat had found a new owner after fetching £22,000 in a charity auction at the end of the 2004/05 season.

Nor was the coat's fame confined to England. In Mourinho's native Portugal sculptor Jose Coelho spent six months making a life-size iron replica of the garment. The 60-kilo sculpture, called 'Soul Overcoat', went on show in a museum in Lisbon in October 2005.

— MISTAKEN IDENTITY —

In the second half of Chelsea's 5–1 defeat at Tottenham in the Worthington Cup semi-final second leg on 23 January 2002 referee Mark Halsey sent off Blues striker Jimmy Floyd Hasselbaink for violent conduct. After the game Halsey viewed a video of the incident and admitted that Hasselbaink was completely innocent and that he should have sent off Chelsea defender and fellow Dutch international Mario Melchiot instead.

— MOONING BLUES —

- Returning to Chelsea for Eddie Niedzwiecki's testimonial game in May 1989, former fans' favourite David Speedie dropped his shorts in response to chants from the Shed. The Football Association fined him £750, although Chelsea chairman Ken Bates generously picked up the tab.
- After scoring Chelsea's opening goal away to Coventry City in August 1997 Frank Sinclair celebrated by dropping his shorts. Again, the FA took a dim view of the incident and fined Frank £750.

— FORTRESS STAMFORD BRIDGE —

On six occasions Chelsea have gone through a whole league season without being beaten at Stamford Bridge:

Season	P	W	D	L	F	A
1910/11	19	17	2	0	48	7
1976/77	21	15	6	0	51	22
2004/05	19	14	5	0	35	6
2005/06	19	18	1	0	47	9
2006/07	19	12	7	0	37	11
2007/08	19	12	7	0	36	13

The Blues' extraordinary form at the Bridge between 2004–08 saw them set an all-time English record of 86 consecutive undefeated home league games, smashing the previous best of 63 games by Liverpool (1978–81). Chelsea's superb run began with a 2–1 win over Fulham on 20 March 2004 and finally ended on 26 October 2008 when a Jose Bosingwa own goal gifted Liverpool victory at the Bridge.

— SAVED BY THE WAR! —

When World War I broke out it initially had little effect on English football and the 1914/15 season was completed as normal. The campaign was a mixed one for the Blues: on a positive note, Chelsea reached the FA Cup Final for the first time, losing to Sheffield United at Old Trafford; less impressively, the Blues finished second bottom of the First Division and looked set to be relegated along with Tottenham.

However, Chelsea's future and that of all the other English league clubs, was put on hold by events across the Channel. The fighting in Flanders between the allied and German armies had continued throughout the 1914/15 season and showed no signs of abating. In the summer of 1915 the Football League decided it had no choice but to suspend league football until the hostilities ceased.

After the war the Football League was restructured, with the First Division being increased from 20 to 22 clubs. Two extra clubs were required to fill the division, and Chelsea were given a reprieve. The other fortunate club was Arsenal who, despite only having finished fifth in the Second Division in 1914/15, were promoted along with Derby and Preston. The Blues, meanwhile, made the most of their lucky escape, finishing third in the first season after the war (1919/20), the highest position in the club's history at that point.

— MOST BIZARRE TV APPEARANCE —

Teddy Maybank, an occasional striker at the Bridge between 1975 and 1977, appeared on ITV's Saturday primetime show *Blind Date* some years after leaving Chelsea.

— CAN WE PLAY YOU EVERY WEEK? —

Of the 44 clubs Chelsea have played in the Premier League since it was founded in 1992, the Blues have remained unbeaten against the following 10 teams:

	P	W	D	L	F	A
Portsmouth	14	13	1	0	32	3
Crystal Palace	8	6	2	0	18	5
Stoke City	8	6	2	0	17	3
Reading	4	3	1	0	6	3
Hull City	4	2	2	0	6	3
Barnsley	2	2	0	0	8	0
Blackpool	2	2	0	0	7	1
Burnley	2	2	0	0	5	1
Swindon Town	2	2	0	0	5	1
Swansea City	2	1	1	0	5	2

— CAPTAIN FANTASTIC —

Current Blues captain John Terry has skippered the side on a record 421 occasions, first taking the armband against Charlton on 5 December 2001. Terry took this particular record from 1970s captain Ron Harris, who led the team out 324 times, while Dennis Wise is in third place, wearing the armband for 298 games.

— FOOTBALLERS' DAUGHTERS CALLED 'CHELSEA' —

Beatrice Chelsea Petrescu, daughter of Dan (Chelsea 1995–2000)
Chelsea Smethurst, daughter of Derek (Chelsea 1970–71)
Chelsea Johnston, daughter of Craig (ex-Liverpool)
Chelsea Merson, daughter of Paul (ex-Arsenal)
Chelsea Pearce, daughter of Stuart (ex-Nottingham Forest)

— THE NAME'S THE SAME —

A number of Chelsea players share their names with other people who are famous in their own field:

Name	Chelsea player	Alternative identity
Steve Francis	80s goalkeeper	US basketball player
Ron Harris	1970 FA Cup skipper	US pro wrestler
David Lee	90s defender	Nobel Prize-winning physicist
John Phillips	70s goalkeeper	Mamas & the Papas member
Graham Roberts	Late 80s captain	*Archers* actor
John Spencer	Tiny 90s striker	70s snooker star
Graham Stuart	Early 90s midfielder	Conservative MP
John Terry	Current skipper	Actor in *ER* and *24*
Mickey Thomas	80s cult hero	Singer with Jefferson Starship
Kevin Wilson	Moustachioed 80s striker	Aussie comedy singer, nicknamed 'Bloody'

— GEORGE'S BARREN RUN —

In the days of baggy shorts, steel-capped boots and laced-up balls, defenders weren't expected to do anything else except defend. Right-back George W Smith, who played for the Blues in the 1920s, took this philosophy to the extreme by failing to score a single goal in 370 games for the club. No other outfield Chelsea player – yes, not even Robert Fleck or Chris Sutton – has been so unprolific in front of goal.

— BLUES ON THE SMALL SCREEN —

Aside from the normal football programmes, references to Chelsea FC have popped up in numerous TV shows, including:

- *Hancock's Half Hour*, BBC1, 1959
  In an episode of the popular 1950s sitcom Tony Hancock follows his local club, East Cheam United, to Stamford Bridge for an encounter with Chelsea, desperately hoping for the draw he needs to scoop the pools jackpot. With United winning 3–1 at half-time Hancock blags his way into the away dressing room, passing himself off as a new club director. He promptly instructs the team to adopt some ridiculous tactics, like putting their smallest player in goal. Sure enough, Chelsea come back to level at 3–3, allowing Hancock

to dream of a new life as a millionaire. His hopes are soon crushed, though, as the Blues take advantage of their opponents' disarray to win 15–3.

- *Minder*, ITV, 1980
  An episode entitled 'All About Scoring, Innit?' has a definite football them, with Terry (Dennis Waterman) looking after a runaway pro player, Danny Varrow (played by Karl Howman), who wants to sell his 'exclusive story' of raunchy affairs and problem gambling to the tabloid press. In one scene Terry attends an actual match at Stamford Bridge – a 1–1 draw with Preston North in the old Second Division on 20 September 1980 – and is shown standing in the Shed. In the end Varrow is sold to a Dutch club, much to the irritation of Terry's boss Arthur Daley (George Cole) who, once again, misses out on 'a nice little earner'.

- *Building Sights*, BBC2, 1995
  In a series of short programmes about architects' favourite buildings, Chelsea supporter Nigel Coates waxes lyrical about the East stand. "The stand is expectant even when it's empty," he muses, while sitting in a deserted upper tier. "The roof is just flying straight out – it's leaping out like a panther towards the pitch."

- *MacIntyre Undercover*, BBC1 1999
  Posing as a hardcore Blues fan complete with the club badge tattoed on his arm, reporter Donal MacIntyre befriends a group of alleged Chelsea football hooligans. Despite much bravura talk in pubs around Stamford Bridge and in journeys to away matches, the film features remarkably little actual violence. Nonetheless, the police take an interest and two members of the gang later receive lengthy prison sentences for conspiracy to commit violent disorder and affray.

- *EastEnders*, BBC1 2006
  New character Kevin Wicks, played by real-life Chelsea fan Phil Daniels, arrives on Albert Square and is soon raising a glass to the Blues, "the world's greatest football team", in that West Ham stronghold, The Queen Vic. In another scene, Kevin is surprised by his aunt, Pat Butcher, while strolling around her living room in a pair of Chelsea boxer shorts. According to Daniels, he only agreed to take the part if his character could be a Chelsea fan.

- *Extras*, BBC2 2006
  In an episode featuring Jonathan Ross, Robert Lindsay and Robert De Niro, Ricky Gervais' character, Andy, and his friend Maggie

visit a sick boy in hospital. When they arrive the boy is lying in bed, covered by a giant duvet featuring the Chelsea club badge. Rather unnecessarily, Maggie asks him, "Are you a Chelsea fan?"

- *Ruddy Hell! It's Harry and Paul*, BBC1 2007
  The comedy show starring Harry Enfield and Paul Whitehouse featured a weekly sketch in which Whitehouse played Roman Abramovich. In one scene, Abramovich and his two minders are approached by a Chelsea-supporting father and son in a park. Abramovich announces that he would like the boy to play with his own son and tells the father, "I buy. How much?" Initially, the father is bemused by the offer but when he is presented with a hefty cheque by one of the minders he heads off in the opposite direction, leaving his bewildered son with the Russians.

  In another regular sketch, Whitehouse appeared as egotistical Premiership manager Jose Arrogantio, whose post-match interviews are a masterclass in referee bashing. Any resemblance to another manager called 'Jose' was, presumably, entirely intentional.

— INTERNATIONALS ALL —

Chelsea first fielded a side entirely made up of internationals away to Coventry City on 15 August 1998. The Blues' team lined up as follows: De Goey (Holland); Ferrer (Spain), Desailly (France), Leboeuf (France), Le Saux (England); Poyet (Uruguay), Wise (England), Di Matteo (Italy), Babayaro (Nigeria); Vialli (Italy), Casiraghi (Italy). Both playing substitiutes, Flo (Norway) and Zola (Italy) were also internationals. Despite this impressive line-up, Chelsea still lost the match 2–1.

— HAT-TRICK RECORD FOR YOUTHFUL GREAVSIE —

When Jimmy Greaves scored his first hat-trick for Chelsea, hitting four goals in the 7–4 home defeat of Portsmouth on Christmas Day 1957, he was aged 17 years and 10 months and the youngest-ever player to score three or more times in the English top flight. Greavsie's record stood for another 31 years until April 1988 when Alan Shearer notched a hat-trick for Southampton against Arsenal, aged 17 years and 240 days.

— CHELSEA MONOPOLY —

In 2005 Chelsea launched its own version of the popular board game Monopoly. Instead of Mayfair, Park Lane and the Old Kent Road, players can purchase former and current Blues and different parts of Stamford Bridge. Sample prices, which tend towards the low side, include:

Petr Cech £60
John Terry £160
Dennis Wise £200
Matthew Harding Stand £200
Kerry Dixon £260
Peter Osgood £300
Gianfranco Zola £350
Jose Mourinho £400

— THORNS IN OUR SIDE —

Just two opposition players have scored five goals against Chelsea in a single game. The first striker to go nap against the Blues was Everton legend 'Dixie' Dean, who filled his boots in a 7–2 thrashing of the west Londoners at Goodison on 14 November 1931.

Then, towards the end of the 1964/65 season, Burnley's beefy centre-forward Andy Lochhead took advantage of a weakened Chelsea line-up to slam five goals past Peter Bonetti in a 6–2 win for the Clarets at Turf Moor.

— 100% LEAGUE RECORD —

Chelsea have won every league encounter against just two clubs, Northampton Town and Brighton & Hove Albion. The Blues beat Northampton 3–2 at the County Ground and 1–0 at the Bridge on consecutive days over Christmas 1965, during the Cobblers' one-season stint in the top flight.

Chelsea had to wait until the 1983/84 season before meeting Brighton in the league for the first time, and triumphed in both encounters – 2–1 at the Goldstone Ground and 1–0 at the Bridge. Five years later the sides clashed again in the old Second Division, Chelsea winning 2–0 at home and 1–0 away.

— ISRAEL? ER, COUNT ME OUT . . . —

In October 2001 Chelsea visited Hapoel Tel Aviv in the Uefa Cup second round, without six first-team regulars who refused to travel to Israel because of concerns about their security in the wake of the terrorist attacks on America on 11 September 2001.

The six players who stayed at home – captain Marcel Desailly, Emmanuel Petit, Eidur Gudjohnsen, Graeme Le Saux, William Gallas and Albert Ferrer – were accused of being 'cowards' by the media, with Desailly coming in for particular criticism after he explained that he couldn't make the trip because he had an ankle injury "linked to toothache".

Although the Israeli Tourism Minister was assassinated by Palestinian militants in Jerusalem the day before the match, Chelsea's party returned from the Holy Land unscathed. A weakened Blues side, though, went down to a 2–0 defeat in Tel Aviv and, despite fielding a full-strength team in the second leg at Stamford Bridge, Chelsea went out of the competition after only managing a draw in the return.

— A PAIR OF KINGS AT THE BRIDGE —

On 21 February 1920 King George V attended the third round FA Cup tie between Chelsea and Leicester City at the Bridge. After meeting the teams and war veterans before the match, His Majesty settled down to watch the Blues beat the Foxes 3–0.

Two weeks later Chelsea again hosted Royalty when the King of Spain, Alfonso XIII, attended the quarter-final FA Cup tie between the Blues and Bradford Park Avenue. Chelsea won the game 4–1 in front of a crowd of 61,223.

— HILLY'S DOUBLE HAT-TRICK —

Chelsea's first goalscoring superstar, striker George 'Gatling Gun' Hilsdon, remains the only player in the club's history to have hit a double hat-trick. George's 'super six' came in the Blues' 9–1 demolition of Midland League side Worksop in the FA Cup first round on 11 January 1908. Five players, including Hilsdon, have scored five goals in a match for Chelsea and they are . . .

Year	Player	Result
1906	George Hilsdon	Chelsea 9 Glossop 2
1958	Jimmy Greaves	Chelsea 6 Wolves 2
1959	Jimmy Greaves	Preston 4 Chelsea 5
1961	Jimmy Greaves	Chelsea 7 WBA 1
1966	Bobby Tambling	Aston Villa 2 Chelsea 6

| 1971 | Peter Osgood | Chelsea 13 Jeunesse Hautcharage 0 |
| 1989 | Gordon Durie | Walsall 0 Chelsea 7 |

— TATTOO BLUE —

Chelsea players whose bodies are adorned by tattoos include:

Joey Jones: Somewhat at variance with his tough guy image, the hard-tackling defender always wore a long-sleeved shirt during his spell at Chelsea in the early 1980s. The reason? Hidden by his blue shirt was a tattoo of a liver bird on his arm, a reminder of Jones' European Cup-winning days at Liverpool.

Vinnie Jones: At the last count the footballer-turned-actor had five separate tattoos: a red rose on his left forearm; an image of the FA Cup marking his win with Wimbledon in 1988; a Leeds club crest commemorating his Second Division title success with the Yorkshire outfit in 1990; a Welsh dragon and feathers on his chest; and, finally, one listing the names of his immediate family in the middle of his shoulders.

Mateja Kezman: He sported an image of Christ on his right arm, but if the Serbian striker prayed for divine intervention to help him find the net at Chelsea, the Almighty clearly wasn't listening.

Juan Sebastian Veron: The onetime Argentina captain has a tattoo of radical revolutionary and fellow countryman Che Guevara on his right arm. Right on!

Gianluca Vialli: He reached the heights with the Blues, just like the soaring eagle tattoo that is perched on his right shoulder.

Raul Meireles: Much of the Portuguese midfielder's body is covered with tattoos, the most eye-catching one being a huge dragon on his back.

Fernando Torres: The Spanish striker's tattoos include a number nine on the inside of his right arm, his wife's name ('Olalla') on the outside of his left arm and a squiggly one on the inside of his left arm, which reads 'Fernando' in tengwar, a script invented by the writer J.R.R. Tolkien.

— CHELSEA COMEDY NAMES XI —

1. Les Fridge (1986)
2. William Dickie (1919–21)
3. Joseph Spottiswood (1920)
4. Jimmy Argue (1933–46)
5. Peter Proudfoot (1906–07)
6. Wilfred Chitty (1932–38)
7. Peter Feely (1971–72)

8. Alan Dicks (1952–57)
9. Jack Cock (1919–22)
10. Mike Brolly (1973–74)
11. Charles Dyke (1948–51)
Manager: Dave Sexton (1967–74)

— HONOURS LIST —

The following Chelsea men have been awarded military or civilian honours:

Jack Cock MM (Military Medal, World War I)
Colin Hampton MM (Military Medal, World War I)
Tom Logan MM (Military Medal, World War I)
Harry Wilding MM (Military Medal, World War I)
Arthur Wileman MM (Military Medal, World War I)
Tommy Walker OBE (1960)
Geoff Hurst MBE (1979), Knighted (1998)
Ron Greenwood CBE (1981)
John Hollins MBE (1982)
Ray Wilkins MBE (1993)
Len Casey MBE (1994)
Mark Hughes MBE (1998), OBE (2004)
Dario Gradi MBE (1998)
Alan Birchenall MBE (2002)
Paul Elliott MBE (2003)
Gianfranco Zola OBE (Honorary, 2004)
Dave Sexton OBE (2005)

— FIRST INTERNATIONAL —

The first player to be capped for his country while playing for Chelsea was left-winger Johnny Kirwan. A member of the very first Blues team, Kirwan won four caps for Northern Ireland in 1906, making his debut in a 5–0 defeat against England in Belfast.

Among the other home countries, Chelsea's first internationals were: George Hilsdon (England, 1907), Jack Cameron (Scotland, 1909), Evan Jones (Wales, 1910) and Dick Whittaker (Republic of Ireland, 1959).

— EURO FINAL AT THE BRIDGE —

On 5 March 1958 Stamford Bridge hosted the first-ever final of the Fairs Cup (later to become the UEFA Cup). The match, which was the first of two legs, was between a London Select XI and Barcelona and finished in a 2–2 draw. Three Chelsea players, Jimmy Greaves, Peter Sillett and Bobby Smith, played for the Londoners, with Greaves scoring one of the goals for the home team. Barcelona won the return 6–0 in the Nou Camp to take the trophy.

— LOCAL TALENT —

The West Stand at Stamford Bridge has six suites which are used for a variety of functions during the week and for corporate entertainment on matchdays. The suites were originally named after famous local residents, but in 2005 were re-named after legendary Chelsea players or, in Ted Drake's case, a onetime manager of the club:

Current name	Formerly named after
The Bonetti Suite	William Wilberforce, anti-slave trade campaigner (1759–1833)
The Clarke Suite	Augustus John, painter (1878–1961)
The Drake Suite	Hilaire Belloc, writer and poet (1870–1953)
The Harris Suite	Charles Kingsley, writer (1819–75)
The Hollins Suite	Captain Scott, Antarctic explorer (1868–1912)
The Tambling Suite	Sylvia Pankhurst, suffragette (1882–1960)

— THE NUMBERS GAME —

Chelsea, along with Arsenal, were the first English club to wear numbered shirts, adopting an idea developed by Gunners boss Herbert Chapman for a home game against Swansea Town on 25 August 1928. The innovation seemed to suit the Blues, who smashed four goals past Swans keeper Alex Ferguson (no relation to the cantankerous Manchester United manager) while keeping a clean sheet at the other end.

The football authorities were opposed to the innovation, however, and the experiment was not repeated until 1933 when numbered shirts were used for the FA Cup Final between Everton and Manchester City. Eventually, in 1939, the Football League made shirt numbers obligatory.

— THRASHED, WALLOPED AND TONKED —

Chelsea's biggest-ever wins in the Premier League:

Date	Result
9 May 2010	Chelsea 8 Wigan Athletic 0
25 April 2010	Chelsea 7 Stoke City 0
27 March 2010	Chelsea 7 Aston Villa 1

16 Jan 2010	Chelsea 7 Sunderland 2
24 Aug 1997	Barnsley 0 Chelsea 6
27 Oct 2007	Chelsea 6 Manchester City 0
14 Aug 2010	Chelsea 6 West Brom 0
21 Aug 2010	Wigan Athletic 0 Chelsea 6
6 Dec 1997	Tottenham 1 Chelsea 6
21 Oct 2000	Chelsea 6 Coventry City 1
12 March 2008	Chelsea 6 Derby County 1
29 April 2012	Chelsea 6 QPR 1
16 March 1997	Chelsea 6 Sunderland 2
1 March 1998	Chelsea 6 Crystal Palace 2

— TOP CAPS —

The ten players to have won the most international caps while with the Blues are:

Player	Country	Caps won with Chelsea
1. Frank Lampard	England	88 caps
2. Marcel Desailly	France	74 caps
3. Didier Drogba	Ivory Coast	72 caps
John Terry	England	72 caps
5. Petr Cech	Czech Republic	65 caps
6. Ricardo Carvalho	Portugal	57 caps
7. Paulo Ferreira	Portugal	48 caps
William Gallas	France	48 caps
Salomon Kalou	Ivory Coast	48 caps
10. Claude Makelele	France	47 caps

— SIGNED FROM SCOTLAND XI —

Until the game north of the border fell into the doldrums, Chelsea had a long history of signing players from Scottish clubs. Here's a sample team:

1. Bill Robertson (signed from Arthurlie, 1946)
2. Steve Clarke (St Mirren, 1987)
3. Andy Dow (Dundee, 1993)
4. Joe McLaughlin (Morton, 1983)
5. Paul Elliott (Celtic, 1991)
6. Doug Rougvie (Aberdeen, 1984)
7. Pat Nevin (Clyde, 1983)
8. Eamonn Bannon (Hearts, 1979)

9. John Spencer (Rangers, 1992)
10. Gordon Durie (Hibernian, 1986)
11. Charlie Cooke (Dundee, 1966)
Manager: Eddie McCreadie (East Stirling, 1962)

— DYNAMIC ATTRACTION —

On 13 November 1945 Chelsea played Moscow Dynamo in a friendly match which, despite being played on a Tuesday afternoon, attracted an enormous crowd to Stamford Bridge. An incredible 74,496 paying customers passed through the turnstiles, but many thousands more entered the ground without paying, clambering over gates and walls to get in, and then swarming onto the greyhound track surrounding the pitch to get a close-up view of the clash between representatives of the wartime allies against Nazi Germany. Other fans burst into houses overlooking the ground, desperate to get even the slightest of glimpses of the game, which finished in an exciting 3–3 draw.

Chelsea striker Tommy Lawton later described the chaotic scenes outside the ground: "When I arrived at Stamford Bridge it seemed as if everybody in London had taken the afternoon off to see the Russians. A huge surging mob were storming the gates and mounted police moved slowly among them trying to restore some semblance of order."

Unofficial estimates put the size of the crowd at around 100,000, easily surpassing Chelsea's official record crowd of 82,905 for a First Division match. Meanwhile, the full list of attendance records at Stamford Bridge is:

Competition	Year	Attendance	Result	
Football League	1935	82,905	Chelsea 1	Arsenal 1
FA Cup	1911	77,952	Chelsea 3	Swindon 1
League Cup	1971	43,330	Chelsea 3	Tottenham 2
Full Members Cup	1990	15,061	Chelsea 2	Crystal Palace 0
Premier League	2004	42,328	Chelsea 4	Newcastle 0
Europe	1966	59,541	Chelsea 2	AC Milan 1

— CHELSEA'S FIRST MATCH —

Chelsea played their first-ever match away to Stockport County in the Second Division on 2 September 1905. By all accounts, the Edgeley Park pitch was in poor condition, with one reporter describing it as "an almost unbroken expanse of ripe plantation weed in full seed."

After a goalless first half, Stockport were given the chance to take the lead when the referee awarded a penalty kick for a foul on one of their forwards. However, Willie Foulke, Chelsea's giant goalkeeper and captain, saved the kick and then threw the ball out to a team-mate. Perhaps, he should have kicked it, as the following contemporary report describes what happened next:

"It pitched on to one of the numerous lumps and deviated sharply to the right. Foulke took the only course open to him and charged from his goal, but Stockport inside-forward, George Dodd, reached the ball first banging it straight at Robert McEwan, who would have cleared it easily but for the fact that Tommy Miller was knocked into him by a County forward at the same time, and as a result the ball glanced off McEwan's chest into the net."

Despite the suggestion of a foul, the goal was given and credited to Dodd. It remained the only goal of the game – and Chelsea's first match ended in defeat.

— CHELSEA OLD BOYS —

Currently managed by 1980s defender Gary Chivers, Chelsea Old Boys play charity matches throughout the year at grounds in the London area and beyond. The side is largely made up of evergreen players from the seventies and eighties, including Ray Wilkins, Garry Stanley and Clive Walker, although younger players such as David Lee, Jason Cundy and Gareth Hall have recently emerged from the club's 'youth academy'.

In 2004 the Old Boys enjoyed their greatest success to date when they won the Build Center Masters Cup in Sheffield, beating Wolves 2–1 in the final thanks to two goals by Kevin Wilson.

The club has its own section on the official website (www.chelseafc. com) where fans can find out more about the players who make up the Old Boys and even challenge them to a match.

— SLAYER OF THE WOLVES —

Didier Drogba and Roy Bentley, Chelsea's first championship-winning captain in 1955, jointly hold the Blues' record for the most goals against another club, with a total haul of 13 against Arsenal and Wolves respectively. Bentley's achievement is perhaps the more impressive considering that the Molineux outfit were the greatest team of the era, winning the league title three times during the 1950s. Wolves, though, never managed to shackle Bentley, as this list of his goals against them proves:

Date	Result	Bentley goals
11 Dec 1948	Chelsea 4 Wolves 1	2
7 May 1949	Wolves 1 Chelsea 1	1

29 Oct 1949	Wolves 2 Chelsea 2	1
25 April 1951	Chelsea 2 Wolves 1	1
22 Sept 1951	Wolves 5 Chelsea 3	1
27 Sept 1952	Chelsea 1 Wolves 2	1
18 Feb 1953	Wolves 2 Chelsea 2	1
26 Sept 1953	Wolves 8 Chelsea 1	1
13 Feb 1954	Chelsea 4 Wolves 2	2
4 Dec 1954	Wolves 3 Chelsea 4	2

— SHIRT SWAP —

Since squad numbers were first introduced at the start of the 1993/94 season the various numbers have become associated with particular Chelsea players. For instance, John Terry has always been number 26, while Gianfranco Zola made the number 25 his own.

At the opposite end of the scale, midfielder Jody Morris appeared in four different shirt numbers (23, 21, 28 and 20) between 1996 and 2003. Six players, meanwhile, have turned out for the Blues in three different shirt numbers:

Player	First shirt no.	Second shirt no.	Third shirt no.
Craig Burley (1993–97)	24	12	14
Steve Clarke (1993–98)	12	2	6
Michael Duberry (1994–99)	28	26	12
David Lee(1993–98)	4	25	15
Andy Myers (1993–99)	3	15	8
Sam Hutchinson (2007–)	51	41	27

— LEAGUE OF NATIONS —

Internationals from the following 47 countries have been on Chelsea's books: All Ireland, Argentina, Australia, Austria, Belgium, Brazil, Cameroon, CIS, Croatia, Czech Republic, Denmark, England, Finland, France, Germany, Georgia, Ghana, Holland, Iceland, Israel, Italy, Ivory Coast, Jamaica, Liberia, Morocco, New Zealand, Nigeria, Northern Ireland, Norway, Peru, Phillipines, Portugal, Republic of Ireland, Russia, Scotland, Serbia, Serbia and Montenegro, Slovakia, South Africa, Spain, Sweden, Switzerland, Turkey, Ukraine, Uruguay, USA and Wales.

— COUNT THE CROWD —

Chelsea's Second Division match with Orient on 5 May 1982 was attended by just 6,009 fans, the lowest gate for a league game at the Bridge since the war. Other all-time attendance lows include:

Year	Competition	Result	Crowd att
1905	FA Cup	Chelsea 6	5,000
		Ist Battalion Grenadiers 1	
1906	Football League	Chelsea 4 Lincoln 2	3,000
1960	League Cup	Chelsea 4 Workington 2	5,630
1991	Full Members Cup	Chelsea 1 Luton 1	3,849
1994	Premiership	Chelsea 1 Coventry 2	8,923

— CHELSEA'S FIRST EVER LINE UP, V STOCKPORT COUNTY (AWAY), 2 SEPTEMBER 1905 —

Goalkeeper: Willie Foulke (captain)
Right-back: Robert Mackie
Left-back: Robert McEwan
Right-half: George Key
Centre-half: Bob McRoberts
Left-half: Tommy Miller
Outside-right: Martin Moran
Inside-right: John Tait Robertson
Centre-forward: David Copeland
Inside-left: Jimmy Windridge
Outside-left: John Kirwan

— OTHER SPORTS STAGED AT STAMFORD BRIDGE —

American Football
Athletics
Baseball
Cricket
Cycling
Greyhound racing
Midget car racing
Rugby league
Rugby union
Speedway

— OI, FANCY A GAME, THEN? —

Current Football League clubs Chelsea have never played in a competitive fixture:

AFC Wimbledon*
Aldershot Town
Burton Albion
Cheltenham Town
Crawley Town
Dagenham & Redbridge
Fleetwood Town
MK Dons
Morecambe
Stevenage
Torquay United
Yeovil Town

* Chelsea played 30 times against Wimbledon, the predecessors of AFC Wimbledon

— BAD DAY AT THE BRIDGE —

Over the years Chelsea supporters have endured some grim afternoons at the Bridge, none more so than when Notts County thrashed the Blues 6–0 on their home patch on 9 February 1924 – the club's biggest home defeat. Unsurprisingly, perhaps, Chelsea ended that particular season by being relegated to the Second Division.

The Blues' worst home defeat in cup competitions was a 4–0 thrashing by Birmingham City in the FA Cup on 14 February 1953 – now that's what you call a Saint Valentine's day massacre.

— CAN WE PLAY YOU EVERY DAY? —

In 1964 Tommy Docherty's Chelsea side went on a post-season tour of the Caribbean, playing a series of fairly undemanding games against local opposition as well as a number of games against fellow tourists Wolves. In fact, the two English teams must have been sick of the sight of each other as they met no fewer than five times in the space of two weeks. The results of these games, and the exotic venues, are given below:

Date	Result	Venue
23 May	Chelsea 1 Wolves 3	Barbados

27 May	Chelsea 3 Wolves 2	Trinidad
29 May	Chelsea 2 Wolves 4	Jamaica
2 June	Chelsea 3 Wolves 0	Jamaica
6 June	Chelsea 2 Wolves 0	Haiti

— ON THE BRINK —

Chelsea have had a few narrow escapes from relegation but none as tight as the one the Blues pulled off in 1951. With four games to go the Londoners were stuck at the bottom of the First Division, four points behind Sheffield Wednesday (21st) and six behind Everton (20th). The trap door to the Second Division was beckoning.

Remarkably, though, the Blues managed to win their next three fixtures at home to Liverpool (1–0) and Wolves (2–1) and away to Fulham (2–1) to move level on points with Wednesday and to within two points of Everton. On the final day of the season Chelsea beat Bolton 4–0 at the Bridge, while Everton, who only needed a draw, were thrashed 6–0 at Hillsborough. With all three teams level on 32 points, goal average was required to separate the teams and Chelsea narrowly came out on top:

First Division bottom three 1950/51

	P	W	D	L	F	A	Pts	GA
20 Chelsea	42	12	8	22	53	65	32	0.815
21 Sheffield Weds	42	12	8	22	64	83	32	0.771
22 Everton	42	12	8	22	48	86	32	0.558

— MYSTIC DAVE —

In January 1970, just before the FA Cup third round, Chelsea manager Dave Sexton was asked by *The Times* to name the clubs he thought would do well in the competition. Sexton's reply showed how confident he was in the squad he had assembled over the previous three seasons:

> *"May I give Chelsea as the winners? We have gone close so often, I believe it's our turn. We are going well at the right time; confidence is sky-high, and (John) Hollins and (Alan) Hudson are now reliable midfield dynamos. With a solid defence, we are also not finding it difficult to score. There is skill on the ground, height near goal to knock in the crosses, and we can play in any conditions."*

Sexton's prediction was spot on, as the Blues went on to win the cup a few months later. His detailed assessment of his team was also uncannily accurate: Chelsea scored a club record 25 goals during their cup run; three of their four goals in the two-match final against Leeds came from headers; and the Blues had to play on a variety of surfaces on their path to glory, including a heavily sanded Wembley pitch in the final. Just about the only thing Sexton's crystal ball got wrong concerned Alan Hudson: the 'reliable midfield dynamo' missed out on a cup winners' medal thanks to an ankle injury.

— TOURING SOUTH AMERICA —

In 1929 Chelsea became one of the first British clubs to visit South America, spending six weeks in Argentina, Brazil and Uruguay. Results were mixed and so, too, were the reviews Chelsea received. After one bruising encounter in Brazil, the Blues were criticised for "displaying inferior technique, in a sporting and social sense". However, a newspaper reporter in Buenos Aires stressed that "Chelsea's record in Argentina was one of keen, honest play, and that any differences of opinion has arisen as the result purely and simply of divergence in the interpretation of the rules that govern the British game of soccer."

What is clear is that the tour helped boost morale at the club and it may not be a coincidence that in the season following the exotic trip Chelsea were promoted to the First Division after six years' absence.

— CITY OF GOALS —

Chelsea players have scored more hat-tricks against Manchester City than any other club. In total, Blues strikers have notched six trebles against the Mancunians:

Year	Player	Goals	Result
1933	Hughie Gallacher	3	Man City 1 Chelsea 4
1935	Joe Bambrick	4	Chelsea 4 Man City 2
1937	George Mills	3	Chelsea 4 Man City 4
1960	Jimmy Greaves	3	Chelsea 6 Man City 3
1984	Kerry Dixon	3	Chelsea 4 Man City 1 (Lge Cup)
1986	David Speedie	3	Chelsea 5 Man City 4 (FM Cup)

— PRESENT AND CORRECT —

Blues legends Ron Harris and John Hollins both played in all Chelsea's league games in four different seasons, a club record. Chopper didn't miss a game in 1964/65, 1966/67, 1972/73 and 1974/75, while Holly was an ever-present in 1969/70, 1971/72, 1972/73 and 1973/74.

— DEADLY ENCOUNTER —

On 1 February 1936 Chelsea drew 3–3 against Sunderland at Roker Park. A few days after the game Sunderland's young goalkeeper James Thorpe died. The coroner's verdict read "death from diabetes, the death being accelerated by rough usage during the match".

— ONE-CAP WONDERS —

The following Chelsea players won just a single cap for their respective countries:

Jurgen Macho* (Austria, 2002)
Ken Armstrong (England, 1955)
Fabio Borini* (Italy, 2012)
William Brown* (England,1924)
Jackie Crawford (England, 1931)
Willie Foulke* (England, 1897)
Harold Halse* (England, 1909)
John Hollins (England, 1967)
Percy Humphreys* (England, 1903)
Tommy Meehan (England, 1924)
Joe Payne* (England, 1937)
Seth Plum* (England, 1923)
Ken Shellito (England, 1963)
Alex Stepney* (England, 1968)
Chris Sutton* (England, 1997)
Cecil Allen* (Northern Ireland, 1935)
John Browning* (Scotland, 1914)
Peter Buchanan (Scotland, 1938)
Warren Cummings (Scotland, 2002)
Angus Douglas (Scotland, 1911)
George Henderson* (Scotland, 1904)
George Key* (Scotland, 1902)
Tom Logan* (Scotland, 1913)
Doug Rougvie* (Scotland, 1984)
Dick Whittaker (Rep. Ireland, 1959)
Roger Freestone* (Wales, 2000)

* Cap won with a club other than Chelsea

— NUMBER 12: TWO FIRSTS —

Substitutes weren't introduced to the English game until the start of the 1965/66 season and, three games into that campaign, John Boyle became the first ever Chelsea sub to come off the bench when he replaced George Graham in the Blues' 3–0 defeat of Fulham at Craven Cottage.

The following season, winger Peter Houseman became the first Chelsea substitute to score when he netted against Charlton Athletic in a League Cup tie at Stamford Bridge on 14 September 1966. The Blues won the game 5–2.

— FACIAL FUZZ CHELSEA XI —

Hair we go: David Webb, Charlie Cooke, Alan Hudson and Peter Osgood

1. **Ed de Goey** (70s porn star-style 'tache)
2. **David Webb** (full on bushy beard)
3. **Eddie McCreadie** (Zapata moustache)
4. **Alan Hudson** (luxuriant sideburns, occasional beard)
5. **Mickey Droy** (Desperate Dan stubble)
6. **Marcel Desailly** (whispy chin tufts)
7. **Clive Walker** (strange blonde-hair-and-dark-beard combo)
8. **Kevin Wilson** (sergeant major 'tache)
9. **Mateja Kezman** ('Amish'-style beard but no moustache)
10. **Gianluca Vialli** (classic 90s goatee)
11. **Charlie Cooke** (extravagantly tapered moustache)

Manager: Jose Mourinho (too-busy-to-shave two days' stubble)

— KALOU'S BENCH RECORD —

Chelsea striker Salomon Kalou has played more games as a sub (107) than any other player. The Ivory Coast forward reached the hundred mark of substitute appearances for the Blues when he came off the bench, and scored, for Chelsea in a 3–0 win at Newcastle on 3 December 2011.

— CUP DEFEAT, BUT BLUES STILL PROGRESS —

Strange as it may seem, the Blues once went through to the next round of the FA Cup after losing their previous game. How come? Well, in season 1945/46 FA Cup ties were played over two legs and after beating West Ham 2–0 at the Bridge, Chelsea lost 1–0 at Upton Park in the second leg but still went into the draw for the fifth round.

— SHOW US YOUR MEDALS —

No Chelsea player has won more medals than John Terry. To date, the hard-tackling defender has collected 13 winners' medals with the Blues, his haul being made up of five FA Cups (one as a non-playing substitute in 2000), three Premier League titles, two Carling Cups, two Community Shields and the Champions League in 2012 (despite missing the final against Bayern Munich through suspension he was still presented with a medal). Let's hope he's got a decent safe . . .

— KEEP THE BLUE FLAG FLYING HIGH —

At any Chelsea home match you'll probably see these fan banners hanging from the stands at Stamford Bridge:

Chelsea Our Religion (no wonder attendances are down at church services . . .)

The Only Place To Be Every Other Saturday (that place being – obviously – Stamford Bridge, as described in Suggs's 1997 FA Cup Final song *Blue Tomorrow*)

Super Frankie Lampard (nearly 200 goals for CFC . . . there's surely no quibbling that Lamps really is 'Super')

JT Captain, Leader, Legend (if you don't know who JT is, you're reading the wrong book!)

Matthew Harding's Blue & White Army (a reference to the much-missed Chelsea FC director and benefactor who died in a helicopter crash in 1996)

Bentley's Boys (skipper Roy Bentley's 1955 title-winners are still revered at the Bridge – who says Chelsea have no history?)

Born Is The King (a tribute to the late Peter Osgood, the Blues' star player of the 1960s and 1970s)

John Terry's Blue Army, Chelsea Loyal (there are few one-club players these days, but JT is one)

The Roman Empire (just in case anyone needed reminding that, yes, Chelsea are owned by one Roman Abramovich)

— GLENN'S CUP DREAM —

Shortly before the draw for the third round of the 1994 FA Cup, Chelsea manager Glenn Hoddle had a vivid dream in which the Blues were drawn to play his brother's Carl team, Barnet. Sure enough, when the Bees were pulled out of the hat they were promptly paired with . . . Chelsea!

Barnet's Underhill ground was deemed too small for such a big match, and the tie was switched to Stamford Bridge. Nonetheless, the north London minnows came close to pulling off a major upset, having the better chances in a 0–0 draw. The Blues, though, made no mistake in the replay, crushing the Bees 4–0.

— PRINCESS MARGARET – A SECRET BLUE? —

Before the 1970 FA Cup Final between Chelsea and Leeds at Wembley, the Royal guest of honour, the late Princess Margaret was introduced to Blues skipper Ron Harris. "While we were chatting she said she hoped Chelsea would win," Ron said later.

As it turned out, Princess Margaret couldn't have been much of a Chelsea fan as she didn't bother attending the replay at Old Trafford, leaving the cup to be presented to Chopper by the President of the Football Association. On the seven occasions Chelsea have won the cup the trophy has been presented by:

FA Cup-winning year	Chelsea captain	Cup presented by
1970	Ron Harris	Dr Andrew Stephen
1997	Dennis Wise	HRH Duke of Kent
2000	Dennis Wise*	HRH Duke of Kent
2007	John Terry	Prince William
2009	John Terry	Kofi Annan
2010	John Terry	Prince William
2012	John Terry	Jimmy Armfield

*In 2000, Wise was assisted in collecting the cup by his son, Henry

— CELERY FACT FILE —

A Chelsea tradition has developed for supporters to bring bunches of celery to cup finals the Blues are involved in – a reference, of course, to the famous 'Celery song' whose lyrics, sadly, are a little too risqué to be printed here. Instead, here are some little known facts about the Blues' vegetable of choice:

- Celery (latin name Apium Graveolens) is believed to be the same plant as selinon, which is mentioned in Homer's Odyssey around 850 BC. The English word 'celery' comes from the French 'celeri' which is itself derived from the original ancient Greek.
- The oldest record of the word 'celeri' is in a ninth-century poem written in either Italy or France. The first record of celery being used as a food dates back to seventeenth-century France.
- Originating in the Mediterranean, celery has been grown as a food crop for thousands of years. However, it is more difficult to grow than other vegetables, requiring a longer growing season, lots of water and preferring cooler temperatures. Without proper care, celery stalks can be very dry and stringy.
- Celery is an ideal snack for anyone trying to lose weight because the process of eating it actually consumes more calories than the vegetable itself possesses.
- A number of Chelsea fans have been arrested for throwing celery on the pitch under Section 2 of the Football (Offences) Act 1991. The act states that is an offence "to throw anything at or towards the playing area or any area in which spectators or other persons are or may be."

A lump of celery

— REFFIN' HELL! —

These match officials won't be receiving any Christmas cards from Chelsea fans:

- **David Elleray:** Referee at the 1994 FA Cup Final between Chelsea and Manchester United, Elleray awarded the Reds two penalties in the match. The first, for a foul by Eddie Newton on Denis Irwin, was not controversial but the second, for a bit of tussling between Blues defender Frank Sinclair and Andrei Kanchelskis which took place just outside the box, incensed the Chelsea team. Eric Cantona calmly slotted both penalties past Blues keeper Dmitri Kharine and United went on to win the game 4–0.

- **Anders Frisk:** The Swedish referee was at the centre of a huge row in February 2005 when he took charge of Chelsea's Champions League match against Barcelona in the Nou Camp. Jose Mourinho was outraged when his assistant Steve Clarke told him that he had seen Barcelona boss Frank Rijkaard entering Frisk's room at half-time, and his mood was not improved when Didier Drogba was sent off in the second half of the Blues' 2–1 defeat. Mourinho's suggestion that Frisk had been influenced by Rijkaard landed him a £9,000 fine and two-match ban from Uefa, a penalty imposed after Frisk had announced that he was retiring from refereeing after receiving death threats from a number of Chelsea fans.

- **Graham Poll:** Jose Mourinho first crossed swords with Poll in December 2004, when the high profile Premiership ref allowed Thierry Henry to shoot past Petr Cech from a quickly taken free-kick at Highbury. "I am more than unhappy," complained the Chelsea manager. "I can't say the word that is in my heart and soul. I know the rules and they are the same anywhere in the world." Two years later, Poll again irritated Mourinho when he sent off Blues skipper John Terry at White Hart Lane and allegedly told Chelsea players that "they needed to be taught a lesson." When, at the end of the 2006/07 season, Poll announced his retirement Mourinho appeared relieved, remarking "from season to season, I was more worried every time he was involved in one of our games."

- **Tom Henning Ovrebo:** During the second leg of the Champions League semi-final against Barcelona at Stamford Bridge in 2009 the bald Norwegian referee waved away four Chelsea penalty appeals, at least two of which appeared to be nailed-on spot-kicks. The home side's anger was increased when Andres Iniesta scored in the last minute to put the Spanish side through to the final on the away goals rule. In the press conference afterwards, Blues manager Guus Hiddink described Ovrebo's performance as "the worst I have ever seen', while full-back Jose Bosingwa was even more outspoken, saying "I don't know whether he's a referee or a thief!"

- **Roan Slysko:** The Slovak assistant referee controversially signalled that Luis Garcia's shot had crossed the line in the Blues' 1–0 defeat to Liverpool in the Champions League semi-final second leg at Anfield in April 2005. The decision infuriated Jose Mourinho who railed afterwards that "the linesman scored the goal" and "it was a goal from the moon." Slysko, though, stood his ground, saying "I am 100% convinced it was a goal."

— THE MEN IN BLACK —

After awarding Manchester United two penalties in the 1994 FA Cup Final, David Elleray was guaranteed a hostile reception whenever he returned to Stamford Bridge. Chelsea fans, though, have more reason to remember 1970 Cup Final referee Eric Jennings with fondness – in a physical, at times, brutal match he kept all the players on the pitch and thus played a small part in the Blues' first-ever FA Cup success.

Curiously, Herbert Bamlett, the referee at the Blues' first FA Cup Final, went on to become a football manager, taking charge of Manchester United between 1927 and 1931.

FA Cup Final	Referee
1915 v Sheffield United	Herbert Bamlett (Gateshead)
1967 v Tottenham	Ken Dagnall (Bolton)
1970 v Leeds	Eric Jennings (Stourbridge)
1994 v Manchester United	David Elleray (Harrow)
1997 v Middlesbrough	Steve Lodge (Barnsley)
2000 v Aston Villa	Graham Poll (Tring)
2002 v Arsenal	Mike Riley (Leeds)
2007 v Manchester United	Steve Bennett (Orpington)
2009 v Everton	Howard Webb (Rotherham)
2010 v Portsmouth	Chris Foy (St Helens)
2012 v Liverpool	Phil Dowd (Stoke)

— SUCCESSFUL START —

No Chelsea manger is ever likely to match Gianluca Vialli's record of winning a trophy in only his ninth game in charge of the Blues, the 1998 Coca-Cola Cup Final against Middlesbrough at Wembley. For good measure the Italian won more silverware in just his twentieth match as Blues boss, the 1998 European Cup Winners' Cup Final against Stuttgart.

Somewhat less successful than Vialli was the Blues' longest-serving manager David Calderhead who was in charge of the team for 966 matches between 1907 and 1933 and won precisely nothing.

— OFFSIDE! . . . OR, ER, MAYBE NOT —

On 31 January 1925 Chelsea played an experimental game against Arsenal at Highbury to test out various possible changes to the offside law. In the second half, the number of defending players required to keep an attacking player onside was reduced from three to two, and this change was brought into the laws of the game for the following season.

It appears that the Blues' participation in the Highbury experiment worked to their advantage at the start of the 1925/26 season as they won their first three games, racking up an impressive goals tally of 13 for and one against in the process.

— HOT TICKET —

Seasons in which Chelsea have had the highest average home league attendance among all Football League clubs:

Season	Average attendance at Stamford Bridge
1907/8	32,894
1909/10	30,210
1911/12	27,197
1912/13	35,368
1913/14	36,131
1919/20	41,142
1921/22	39,095
1923/24	32,000
1925/26	34,190
1954/55	48,302

Remarkably, Chelsea were in the Second Division during two of these seasons (1911/12 and 1925/26), while on two other occasions (1909/10 and 1923/24) the crowds still flocked to the Bridge despite these being relegation campaigns. The average attendance during Chelsea's first championship year, 48,302, is the club's highest ever and will not be beaten unless the ground is radically redeveloped.

— THE CAT'S WHISKERS —

During his 19-year Chelsea career (1960–79) the Blues' legendary goalkeeper Peter Bonetti played 729 games for the club, keeping 208 clean sheets. His enduring quality and unfailing consistency helped him see off no fewer than 13 rivals, all of whom played at least one game for Chelsea during Bonetti's undisputed reign as 'Number One':

Goalkeeper	Matches played as Bonetti's understudy	Clean sheets
Reg Matthews+ (1956–61)	8	0
Errol McNally (1961–63)	9	0
John Dunn (1962–66)	16	3
Jim Barron (1965–66)	1	0
Mike Pinner (1961–62)	1	0
Kingsley Whiffen (1966–67)	1	0
Alex Stepney (1966)	1	1
Tommy Hughes (1965–71)	11	1
John Phillips (1970–79)	149	30
David Webb~ (1968–74)	1	1
Steve Sherwood (1971–76)	17	3
Bob Iles* (1978–83)	7	1
Petar Borota* (1979–81)	12	1

+ Also played for Chelsea before Bonetti's debut
~ Normally outfield player
* Also played for Chelsea after Bonetti's retirement

— ONE FOR THE LADIES —

In the summer of 1984 Blues striker Kerry Dixon was voted runner-up in a poll to find Britain's 'dishiest' footballer by the female readers of *Match* magazine.

"His blond hair and lovely brown eyes are enough to send a shiver down my spine," wrote Claire Britton of York, while Katrina Stock of Twickenham reckoned, "He is the nearest thing to a perfect man I have ever seen." But not, it would seem, quite as perfect a specimen of masculinity as the poodle-permed captain of England and Manchester United, Bryan Robson, whose chiselled good looks pushed Kerry into second place.

— SCOUSERS DOUBLED BY HARRY AND JOE —

Chelsea have only ever achieved three league 'doubles' over Liverpool, and in two of those seasons the Blues had the same player to thank. In 1919, Harold Brittan scored the only goal of the match on consecutive weekends to give Chelsea the points against the Reds. Then, in the 2004/05 season, Joe Cole twice came off the bench to net in the Blues' 1–0 wins at the Bridge and up at Anfield.

— BACK IN BLUE . . . AFTER EIGHT YEARS! —

The longest gap between Chelsea appearances is held by John Hollins. In his first spell at the club, the popular midfielder made his last appearance for the Blues in a 1–0 home defeat by Manchester City on 12 April 1975, before joining local rivals QPR. In 1983 Hollins returned to the Bridge as player/coach, making his second debut in a 5–0 thrashing of Derby County on 27 August – an incredible eight years and four months after he had last worn the famous blue shirt.

Remarkably, Hollins's record might easily have been beaten by his 1970s team-mate Alan Hudson, who also went back to Chelsea in the summer of 1983, nine and a half years after his last outing for the Blues on 29 December 1973. However, Hudson failed to make a first-team appearance in his second spell at the Bridge before returning to another of his former clubs, Stoke City.

— BACK-TO-BACK FIXTURES —

Players and managers today often complain about fixture congestion, but in the past it was common for teams to play each other on consecutive days over holiday periods. The last time the Blues played two days running was in March 1986, when they won 1–0 at Southampton on the Saturday thanks to a Colin Pates goal, and then beat Manchester City 5–4 in the Full Members Cup Final at Wembley on the Sunday. Meanwhile, selected head-to-head holiday results include:

Year	Christmas Day	Boxing Day
1912	Chelsea 1 Manchester United 4	Manchester United 4 Chelsea 2
1923	Nottingham Forest 2 Chelsea 0	Chelsea 1 Nottingham Forest 1
1931	Blackpool 2 Chelsea 4	Chelsea 4 Blackpool 1
1946	Chelsea 1 Preston North End 2	Preston North End 1 Chelsea 1
1957	Chelsea 7 Portsmouth 4	Portsmouth 3 Chelsea 0

— HE LOOKS TASTY – SIGN HIM UP! —

Ten players who scored against Chelsea at Stamford Bridge before joining the Blues:

Year	Player	Result
1966	Tony Hateley	Chelsea 0 Aston Villa 2
1978	Colin Lee	Chelsea 1 Tottenham 3
1982	Mick Hazard	Chelsea 2 Tottenham 3
1989	Clive Allen	Chelsea 1 Manchester City 1
1989	Dennis Wise	Chelsea 2 Wimbledon 5
1991	Robert Fleck	Chelsea 0 Norwich City 3
1994	Chris Sutton	Chelsea 1 Blackburn 2
1994	Mark Hughes	Chelsea 2 Manchester United 3
1998	Bjarne Goldbaek	Chelsea 1 FC Copenhagen 1
2005	Michael Ballack	Chelsea 4 Bayern Munich 2

— CHELSEA'S LEADING PREMIERSHIP SCORERS —

1992/93	Mick Harford, Graham Stuart	9 goals
1993/94	Mark Stein	13 goals
1994/95	John Spencer	11 goals
1995/96	John Spencer	13 goals
1996/97	Gianluca Vialli	9 goals
1997/98	Tore Andre Flo, Gianluca Vialli	11 goals
1998/99	Gianfranco Zola	13 goals
1999/2000	Tore Andre Flo, Gustavo Poyet	10 goals
2000/01	Jimmy Floyd Hasselbaink	23 goals
2001/02	Jimmy Floyd Hasselbaink	23 goals
2002/03	Gianfranco Zola	14 goals
2003/04	Jimmy Floyd Hasselbaink	12 goals
2004/05	Frank Lampard	13 goals
2005/06	Frank Lampard	16 goals
2006/07	Didier Drogba	20 goals
2007/08	Frank Lampard	10 goals
2008/09	Nicolas Anelka	19 goals
2009/10	Didier Drogba	29 goals
2010/11	Florent Malouda	13 goals
2011/12	Frank Lampard, Daniel Sturridge	11 goals

— TERRY'S WIND-UP BACKFIRES —

Chelsea captain Terry Venables was so confident that the Blues would win the 1965 FA Cup semi-final against Liverpool at Villa Park that he made a mock programme for the Wembley final with Chelsea listed as one of the finalists. It's not entirely clear whether the programme was designed to wind-up the Liverpool squad or just amuse Venables' team-mates, but a copy found its way into the Liverpool dressing-room, where it was used by manager Bill Shankly as a motivational tool.

"We were sitting in the dressing room before the game when Shankly came in fuming and pinned this brochure to the wall," recalled Reds defender Tommy Smith. "'You won't believe it,' he told us, 'but those cocky lot think they're in the final already. Look! They've made up a mock-brochure for the final!' Shanks was fuming and so were we. We went out there and Chelsea never stood a chance."

Despite having played a tough European Cup tie in Rotterdam just two days earlier, Liverpool were the more dynamic of the two teams and beat the Blues 2–0. Venables' joke programme might have seemed like a good idea at the time, but it was a joke which had badly backfired.

— FA VETO BLUES' EURO ADVENTURE —

In 1955 Chelsea, then reigning English league champions, were invited to take part in the inaugural contest of the European Cup. However, the Football Association were concerned that the new tournament would adversely affect the normal league season and advised Chelsea to withdraw. The Blues, who had already been drawn to play Swedish champions Djurgardens, followed the FA's advice and, as it turned out, had to wait until 1999 before finally taking part in European football's premier competition.

— BLUE PUNDITS —

Ex-Chelsea players who are now working as football pundits:

Craig Burley (Five Live)
Jason Cundy (TalkSport)
Albert Ferrer (Sky Sports)
Ruud Gullit (Sky Sports)
Glenn Hoddle (Sky Sports)
Jakob Kjeldberg (TV3, Denmark)
Pat Nevin (Five Live)

Mickey Thomas (Piccadilly Magic)
Andy Townsend (ITV)
Gianluca Vialli (Sky Italia)
Clive Walker (BBC London)
Ray Wilkins (Sky Sports)

— TOMMY'S LATE ARRIVAL . . . AND PREMATURE DEPARTURE —

On Christmas Day 1920 Chelsea's new signing from Manchester United, wing-half Tommy Meehan, turned up at Stamford Bridge fully expecting to make his debut for his new club against Liverpool. To his dismay, he found that the match, a 1–1 draw, had already been played that morning.

Tragically, Meehan died a few days before the start of the 1924/25 season. A memorial fund for his wife and children raised £1,500 thanks to contributions from 15 other League clubs. The fund was also boosted by a benefit match staged at Stamford Bridge on 20 October 1924 between Chelsea and a Football League XI.

— FINAL SHAME —

Only three Chelsea players have experienced the ignominy of being sent off in a major final. In the 1998 European Cup Winners' Cup Final in Stockholm Dan Petrescu was slightly unfortunate to be dismissed for a foul challenge on a Stuttgart player after 84 minutes. Nine years later, in the 2007 Carling Cup final between Chelsea and Arsenal at the Millennium stadium in Cardiff, John Obi Mikel was sent off after grappling with Gunners defender Kolo Toure. The Arsenal player was also shown the red card along with team-mate Emmanuel Adebayor, who was dismissed for his role in the mass brawl which followed the original incident. Then, the following year, Didier Drogba was sent off in the Champions League Final in Moscow after aiming a slap at Manchester United defender Nemanja Vidic.

— SUBSTITUTE SKIPPER —

At Selhurst Park on 20 November 1971, Chelsea played the first 24 minutes of the match without their skipper, midfielder Steve Kember. Having taken part in the toss, Kember then took up his place on the substitutes' bench and only got involved in the action when he replaced the injured Tommy Baldwin. He then led the Blues to a 3–2 victory against the side he had left just two months earlier.

— HOME FROM HOME —

On two occasions Chelsea have played both the original FA Cup tie and the subsequent replay at Stamford Bridge. In 1915 the Blues were drawn at home to Southern League side Swindon in the first round. After a 1–1 draw, the replay a week later was also staged at the Bridge by mutual agreement, with Chelsea winning 5–2 after extra-time. Then, in 1994, Chelsea's third round away tie with Barnet was switched from the north Londoners' tiny Underhill stadium to Stamford Bridge on safety grounds. The match finished in a 0–0 draw before Chelsea won the replay, again at the Bridge, by a convincing 4–0 margin. Strangely, in both 1915 and 1994 Chelsea went on to finish as FA Cup runners-up.

— STRANGEST GOAL EVER? —

The most bizarre goal scored at Stamford Bridge, and quite possibly in the history of football, occurred during a game between Chelsea and Leicester City on 18 December 1954. In an attempt to clear the ball from their penalty area after John McNichol's shot had hit the bar, Leicester defenders Stan Milburn and Jack Froggatt only managed to send it spinning past their goalkeeper, John Anderson. The goal went down in the record books as 'Milburn and Froggatt shared own goal', the only known occasion when a goal has been credited in this way.

— ENDING THE SEASON ON A HIGH . . . OR A LOW —

Chelsea recorded their biggest-ever last day of the season victory in 2010, thrashing Wigan Athletic 8–0 at Stamford Bridge to clinch the Premier League title and the first leg of 'The Double'. Striker Didier Drogba featured in most of the following day's sports headlines after grabbing three goals in the match.

Less enjoyably for Chelsea fans, the Blues have twice been walloped 5–1 at home on the last day: in 1960 by Wolves and in 1986 by Watford.

— HELLO, GOODBYE —

Ten Chelsea players who were swapped with ten others from rival clubs:

Year	Transferred player	Signed player	To/From
1946	Joe Payne	Harry Medhurst	West Ham
1959	Les Allen	Johnny Brooks	Tottenham
1959	Cliff Huxford	Charlie Livesey	Southampton
1961	Ron Tindall	Andy Malcolm	West Ham

1966	George Graham	Tommy Baldwin	Arsenal
1968	Joe Kirkup	David Webb	Southampton
1984	Tony McAndrew	Darren Wood	Middlesbrough
1992	Tommy Boyd	Tony Cascarino	Celtic
1993	Graeme Le Saux	Steve Livingstone	Blackburn
2006	William Gallas	Ashley Cole	Arsenal

— CHEERS, OLD CHUM! —

Five Chelsea players have scored for the club while not actually being on the pay-roll:

- In May 1978, three years after leaving the Bridge and five years before he returned, John Hollins scored for the Blues while playing for QPR. Chelsea won the game 3–1.
- In October 1984, two years after leaving Chelsea, Mickey Nutton scored for the Blues in their 3–1 defeat of Millwall in the League Cup.
- In February 1992, two years before he signed for Chelsea, Mal Donaghy netted for the Blues while playing for Manchester United in a 1–1 draw at Old Trafford.
- In August 1999, former Chelsea defender Frank Sinclair helpfully headed into his own net in the last minute to earn the Blues a point at Leicester.
- In February 2005, two years before he joined Chelsea, Barcelona defender Juliano Belleti diverted Damien Duff's cross into his own net during the Blues' 2–1 defeat in the Nou Camp in the first leg of a Champions League last 16 tie.

— MEALS ON WHEELS —

In 1977 hungry Blues fans travelling by rail to away matches were able to buy a 'Chelsea snack-pack' consisting of roll, sandwich, sausage roll, fruit and biscuits. The price? A bargain 75p.

— MEDAL-WINNING BOSSES —

The Chelsea managers who won the FA Cup in their playing days are:

David Calderhead (Notts County, 1894)
Ted Drake (Arsenal, 1936)
Danny Blanchflower (Tottenham, 1961 and 1962)
Geoff Hurst (West Ham, 1964)
Eddie McCreadie (Chelsea, 1970)
John Hollins (Chelsea, 1970)

David Webb (Chelsea, 1970)
Ian Porterfield (Sunderland, 1973)
Glenn Hoddle (Tottenham, 1981 and 1982)
Gianluca Vialli (Chelsea, 1997)
Roberto di Matteo (Chelsea, 1997 and 2000)

— CELEBS TURN OUT FOR BLUES IN LA —

During their 2006 American tour, Chelsea hosted a reception at the exclusive Sky Bar in Los Angeles. Among the A-list celebrities spotted chatting to Blues players at the star-studded event were:

Tony Blair, Prime Minister of Great Britain
Snoop Dogg, rapper
Serena and Venus Williams, tennis players
Jennifer Love Hewitt, actress
Brandon Flowers, lead singer with The Killers
Joshua Jackson, Dawson's Creek actor
Rick Fox, captain of the LA Lakers basketball team
Vidal Sassoon, hairdresser to the stars

— FAMILIAR FOE —

Chelsea have played London rivals Arsenal more often than any other club. In all competitions, the two sides have met 177 times since their first encounter at Stamford Bridge in November 1907. Chelsea have won 54 of these matches, Arsenal have recorded 71 victories and there have been 52 draws.

— ZOLA IS GREATEST EVER —

In January 2003 Gianfranco Zola was voted Chelsea's best ever player in a poll of fans on the club's official website. The little Sardinian received a staggering 60 per cent of the votes, to put him a considerable distance ahead of the runner-up, 70s striker Peter Osgood. The top ten, which would presumably look very different if a similar poll was conducted today, was as follows:

1) Gianfranco Zola
2) Peter Osgood
3) Dennis Wise
4) Jimmy Greaves
5) Kerry Dixon
6) Ruud Gullit
7) Peter Bonetti
8) Charlie Cooke
9) Gianluca Vialli
10) Jimmy Floyd Hasselbaink

— OH NO, NOT YOU LOT AGAIN! —

Between 2001 and 2004 Chelsea were drawn to play Arsenal in the FA Cup in four consecutive seasons. The run began in the fifth round in 2001 when, despite a superb goal by Jimmy Floyd Hasselbaink, Arsenal won 3–1 at Highbury. The following year the Gunners beat Chelsea 2–0 at Cardiff in the final and it was déjà vu in 2003 when Arsenal beat the Blues 3–1 at Stamford Bridge in a sixth round replay. Amazingly, in 2004 it was Groundhog Day yet again as the Gunners came from a goal down at half-time to beat Chelsea 2–1 at Highbury in the fifth round. The run finally came to an end in 2005 when Newcastle knocked the Blues out of the FA Cup in a fifth round tie at St James' Park.

— YOUNG PLAYER OF THE YEAR —

1983 Keith Dublin
1984 Robert Isaac
1985 Gareth Hall
1986 Micky Bodley
1987 Jason Cundy
1988 Eddie Cunnington
1989 No award
1990 No award
1991 Andy Myers
1992 Zeke Rowe
1993 Neil Shipperley
1994 Mark Nicholls
1995 Chris McCann
1996 Jody Morris
1997 Nick Crittenden
1998 John Terry
1999 Sam Dalla Bona
2000 Rhys Evans
2001 Leon Knight
2002 Carlton Cole
2003 Robert Huth
2004 Robert Huth
2005 Robert Huth
2006 Lassana Diarra
2007 John Obi Mikel
2008 Under-18 squad
2009 Michael Mancienne
2010 Under-18 squad
2011 Josh McEachran
2012 Lucas Piazon

John Terry is the only player on this list to go on and win the Chelsea Player of the Year award (2001 and 2006) while, at the other end of the achievement scale, Eddie Cunnington, Zeke Rowe, Chris McCann and Rhys Evans failed to make a single first team appearance for the Blues.

— FLYING HIGH —

On 19 April 1957 Chelsea became the first English club to travel by air to a Football League match. The new experience seemed to suit the Blues who won 2–1 at Newcastle with goals from Derek Saunders and Les Stubbs. The following day there was no sign of jet lag either, as Chelsea thrashed Everton 5–1 at the Bridge.

— CHARITY BEGINS AT THE BRIDGE —

In 1908 the first ever Charity Shield match was played at Stamford Bridge, between league champions Manchester United and Southern League champions QPR. After a 1–1 draw, United won the replay 4–0. The matches raised £1,275 for charitable causes.

The following three Charity Shields were also held at the Bridge, which has been the venue for 10 of these games in total. The most recent was in 1970 when FA Cup winners Chelsea lost 2–1 at home to league champions Everton.

— WHAY AYE, I'VE SWAPPED ME TOON SHIRT WITH THAT ZOLA! —

The strange story of how Newcastle United fan Tony Spooner ended up with Gianfranco Zola's Chelsea shirt after the FA Cup semi-final between the two clubs at Wembley on 9 April 2000:

> *"I was clapping the Chelsea lads as they came off. I was with most of the United fans behind the goal at the tunnel end, and Zola caught my eye and indicated he wanted my shirt. I threw it down to him and he took his own off and insisted it was passed to me.*
>
> *I could have sold it a hundred times over at Wembley because Chelsea fans were offering as much as £150 for it, but despite the fact that I can't get into it – I'm extra large and he's only medium – I wouldn't part with it. I've had to buy another black and white shirt to replace the one I gave Zola, so it was an expensive day out . . . but it's a day I'll never forget and, of course, I have something very special to remember it by.*

Overall, though, it was a day to forget for the Newcastle fans as their team went down to a 2–1 defeat, Gus Poyet scoring both goals for Chelsea.

— MUSICAL FANS —

Celebrity Chelsea fans in the music business include:

Bryan Adams
Damon Albarn (Blur)
Lloyd Cole
Paul Cook (Sex Pistols)
Dave Gahan (Depeche Mode)
Geri Halliwell (Spice Girls)
Paul Hardcastle
Morten Harket (A-Ha)
Nik Kershaw
Gary Numan
Suggs (Madness)

— EUROPEAN RECORD —

Before the start of the 2012/13 season, Chelsea had taken part in 21 European campaigns. The first was in 1958/59 when the Blues reached the second round of the Fairs Cup before going out 4–2 on aggregate to Red Star Belgrade. The most successful were in 1970/71 and 1997/98 when Chelsea won the European Cup Winners' Cup, and 2011/12 when the Blues won the Champions League for the first time in their history after defeating Bayern Munich 4–3 on penalties in the final.

For many years the Blues had a proud unbeaten home record in Europe, remaining undefeated at Stamford Bridge for 33 matches (27 wins, 6 draws) between 1958 and 2000. That record was finally ended by Lazio who won 2–1 at the Bridge in a Champions League second group stage match on 22 March 2000. Overall, Chelsea's European record reads:

	P	W	D	L	F	A
Home	89	63	21	5	189	52
Away	91	32	27	32	117	104
Neutral	6	3	3	0	7	4
Total	186	98	51	37	313	160

— THE FIRST FOREIGNER —

Danish international Nils Middelboe was the first player from outside Britain or Ireland to play for Chelsea. A Danish international defender, he came to London on business before World War I and, looking for a club to play for, signed for Chelsea as an amateur in 1913.

'The Great Dane', as he was known, played for the Blues for nine years and became an inspirational captain, although his business interests often meant he was unavailable for selection. Outside wartime friendlies, Middlelboe only made 46 appearances for the club but he made a big impression on his team-mates, who presented him with a silver cigarette box when he returned to Denmark in 1922.

Throughout his time at the Bridge Middelboe refused to accept a penny from the club in return for his services. Asked once by the Chelsea secretary what his expenses were, he replied: "Expenses? I ought to pay the club for providing a fine afternoon's sport."

— A MARATHON AND A SPRINT —

In the 2006/07 season Chelsea played a club record 64 matches: 38 in the Premiership, 12 in the Champions League, seven in the FA Cup, six in the Carling Cup and one in the Community Shield. Midfielder Frank Lampard set a club appearance record by playing in 62 of the games (58 starts plus four as sub).

By contrast, in five pre-World War 1 seasons Chelsea played just 40 matches: 38 in the league and two in the FA Cup.

— A RECORD-BREAKING SEASON 2 —

The last time Chelsea were promoted to the top flight, back in season 1988/89, they went up with a then record number of points for the old Second Division, 99. The Blues' impressive tally stood for 10 years until Sunderland amassed a total of 105 points in 1998/99.

Second Division Top Six 1988/89

	P	W	D	L	F	A	Pts
Chelsea	46	29	12	5	96	50	99
Manchester City	46	23	13	10	77	53	82
Crystal Palace	46	23	12	11	71	49	81
Watford	46	22	12	12	74	48	78
Blackburn Rovers	46	22	11	13	74	59	77
Swindon Town	46	20	16	10	68	53	76

— SPORTY BLUES —

So popular are Chelsea among practitioners of other sports the Blues could almost enter their own Olympic team of celebrity fans. Among the most famous sports people to follow the club are:

Alec Stewart, Graham Thorpe, Shane Warne (Cricket)
Pat Cash, Boris Becker (Tennis)
Jimmy White, Tony Drago (Snooker)
Lawrence Dallaglio, Brian Moore, Sir Clive Woodward (Rugby Union)
Dick Francis, Clare Balding (Horse racing)
Johnny Herbert (Motor racing)
Joe Calzaghe (Boxing)
Eric Bristow (Darts)
Daley Thompson (Athletics)
Sir Steven Redgrave (Rowing)

— HAT-TRICK HEROES —

No fewer than 64 Chelsea players have scored hat-tricks for the Blues, the most recent member of this prestigious club being striker Fernando Torres who scored three times against QPR at the Bridge on 29 April 2012. The most prolific scorer of hat-tricks is legendary hit-man Jimmy Greaves who struck an incredible 13 in just 169 appearances for the Blues – an average of one every 13 games!

Player	Number of hat-tricks	Appearances
Jimmy Greaves	13	169
George Hilsdon	9	164
Bobby Tambling	8	370
Kerry Dixon	8	420
Peter Osgood	5	380

— CHOPPER NOT SO HARD? —

In August 2007 *The Times* published a list of the 50 greatest hard men in football. Only one Chelsea player featured in the list and there are no prizes for guessing that it was 70s hatchetman Ron 'Chopper' Harris.

Chopper, though, can't have been too impressed that he only appeared at number 25, some way below no fewer than four members of the Leeds team who were Chelsea's great rivals of the era: Norman Hunter (18), Billy Bremner (16), Paul Reaney (13) and Johnny Giles (5). Andoni Goikoetxea, the so-called 'Butcher of Bilbao' who famously kicked Diego Maradona out of Spanish football, topped the list.

— EUROPEAN CHAMPS:
REACTION FROM AROUND THE GLOBE —

Chelsea's dramatic triumph in the 2012 Champions League final got everyone talking. Here's a selection of the best quotes:

"Now, at last, we have this cup. It's coming back with us to Stamford Bridge and that's the best feeling ever."

Chelsea goalscoring hero Didier Drogba

"It's been very difficult but to finish like this is an incredible achievement."

Blues boss Roberto di Matteo

"I've been here 11 years and I have been waiting for this baby for a long time. I'm pleased we haven't won it before, because it feels even more special."

Chelsea captain Frank Lampard

"It was destiny for us to win. It was also team spirit and togetherness, put it together and it's a wonderful way for us to win the cup."

Salomon Kalou

"If you told me at the start of the season I would win the Champions League I would think you were joking; it's incredible."

Gary Cahill, who only joined the Blues from Bolton four months earlier

"It's a great success, not only for Chelsea but the whole of English football."

England manager Roy Hodgson

"It's not often you get to watch an England-Germany game with the [German] chancellor, it goes to penalties and England win. So this was a great moment."

British Prime Minister David Cameron, who watched the final with other world leaders during a summit at Camp David

"How much bad luck fits into a single football match?"

A sour grapes headline in Munich daily Suddeutsche Zeitung

"Every English man should be proud of Chelsea! Even Arsenal and Spurs fans!"

Arsenal midfielder Jack Wilshere on Twitter

"Their name was written on it long before today! Congratulations to Chelsea."
Former England striker Michael Owen on Twitter

"Will all the subs and fringe players please leave the trophy alone! Let the chaps lift it. Happy for Lampard and co."
QPR midfielder Joey Barton is unimpressed by the Blues' victory celebrations (on Twitter)

"Eureka moment for Chelsea, Europa moment for Spurs!"
Former England cricket captain and Chelsea fan Alec Stewart can't resist putting the boot in on Tottenham on Twitter

"Looking at them just make me wanna celebrate something with my team as well."
Arsenal defender Bacary Sagna, in envious mood on Twitter

— GOING DOWN, GOING DOWN, GOING DOWN! —

On two occasions Chelsea have relegated teams from the Premiership by beating them at Stamford Bridge on the last day of the season. In 1994 the Blues came from behind to defeat Sheffield United 3–2, thanks to a last-minute Mark Stein goal. The result meant the Blades were relegated instead of Ipswich.

Four years later, in 1998, Chelsea beat Bolton 2–0 at the Bridge to send the Trotters down. The home crowd, though, would have preferred to have seen Everton relegated and chanted "let 'em score!" as Bolton mounted a series of desperate attacks in the closing minutes. Sadly for the Trotters, the Blues' defence ignored the chants.

— TOTTENHAM HOODOO —

Chelsea were unbeaten in 32 league meetings against London rivals Tottenham between 1990 and 2007, their longest such run against any club. The sequence began with a 3–2 victory for the Blues at Stamford Bridge on 1 December 1990 and finally came to an end with a 2–1 defeat at White Hart Lane on 5 November 2007.

Of the 32 games between the clubs during that period Chelsea won 21 and drew 11, scoring 63 goals and conceding just 23 in the process. The Blues' leading scorer during their phenomenal run was Jimmy Floyd Hasselbaink with 10 goals, including a hat-trick in a 4–0 home win over Spurs in March 2002.

— GOALS GALORE 2 —

Although Chelsea have only scored ten or more goals just once in a competitive match, the Blues have hit double figures on a number of occasions in friendlies and unofficial fixtures:

Year	Result	Fixture category
1964	St James (Jamaica) 0 Chelsea 15	Friendly
2001	Cascia (Italy) 0 Chelsea 14	Friendly
1965	Tasmania (Australia) 0 Chelsea 12	Friendly
1964	St Mary's (Jamaica) 1 Chelsea 12	Friendly
2000	Reggioteam (Holland) 0 Chelsea 11	Friendly
1916	Chelsea 11 Luton Town 1	Wartime league
1943	QPR 2 Chelsea 11	Wartime league
1972	Barbados Combined XI 0 Chelsea 10	Friendly
1994	Kingstonian 0 Chelsea 10	Friendly

— CHAIRMAN'S UNSUNG HERO AWARD —

In 1994 Ken Bates established an annual chairman's award for the club's 'unsung hero'. The winners of the award are:

1994 Kevin Hitchcock
1995 David Lee
1996 Gwyn Williams
1997 Terry Byrne
1998 Gustavo Poyet
1999 Gianluca Vialli
2000 Antonio Pintus
2001 Claudio Ranieri
2002 John Terry and Jody Morris

— THE YOUNG WONS —

Chelsea have won the FA Youth Cup on four occasions, in 1960, 1961, 2010 and 2012. Among those who played in at least one of those two earlier finals were played in at least one of these finals were Terry Venables, Bert Murray, Bobby Tambling, Peter Bonetti and Ron Harris, all of whom went on to enjoy long careers with the Blues:

Year	Results
1960	Chelsea 1 Preston North End 1
	Preston North End 1 Chelsea 4 (2–5 on agg)

1961	Chelsea 4 Everton 1
	Everton 2 Chelsea 1 (3–5 on agg)
2010	Aston Villa 1 Chelsea 1
	Chelsea 2 Aston Villa 1 (3–2 on agg)
2012	Chelsea 4 Blackburn Rovers 0
	Blackburn 1 Chelsea (1–4 on agg)

The Blues had a chance to add to these triumphs when they reached the final again in 2008, but they were beaten 4–2 on aggregate by Manchester City.

— COLIN'S RED ARM BAND —

During the 1985/86 season Chelsea skipper Colin Pates broke with convention by wearing a red arm band, rather than a black one. He explained why in the home programme against Fulham in October 1985: "A few people have asked me about the red arm band I've been wearing this season so here's the explanation: some referees have been asking team captains to wear identification this season and as I don't like to wear morbid black, Norman Medhurst (team trainer) made a red arm band for me out of an old sock." However, the old sock got the boot when Pates was replaced as skipper by Joe McLaughlin at the start of the 1987/88 season.

— BIG FISH V SMALL FRY —

Chelsea have played numerous friendlies against non-league opposition over the years. Despite being apparent mismatches, results have not always gone the way of the Blues – as these scores indicate:

1906	Chelsea 0 London Caledonians 1
1924	Chelsea 0 Corinthians 2
1974	Hastings United 2 Chelsea 1
1979	Weymouth 2 Chelsea 1
1981	Woking 2 Chelsea 2
1989	Keynsham Town 0 Chelsea 0
1993	Chesham United 4 Chelsea 1

— YOU ARE THE WEAKEST LINK . . . GOODBYE! —

Two former Chelsea players, Peter Bonetti and Graeme Le Saux, have appeared on the popular TV quiz show *The Weakest Link*. In 2001 Bonetti was one of nine former footballers who braved the acid tongue of presenter

Anne Robinson in a special charity edition of the show. 'The Cat' survived to the last five before being voted off. Martin Chivers, the onetime Tottenham and England striker, won the contest.

In 2005 Graeme Le Saux did even better in a sports stars edition of *The Weakest Link*. He beat off competition from the likes of hurdler Colin Jackson, rower James Cracknell and Grandstand host Steve Rider to reach the final, before losing out to BBC horse racing presenter and Chelsea fan Clare Balding.

— 1970 CUP FINAL SUPERSTITIONS —

The Chelsea squad of 1970 had a number of rituals and superstitions which – who knows? – may have helped them win the FA Cup for the first time in the club's history:

- Manager Dave Sexton carried some wishbones with him for every cup tie. And they weren't just any old wishbones, either – 15 years previously they had belonged to Jim Lewis, Chelsea's inside-left in the club's 1955 League Championship-winning side.
- Blues defender David Webb volunteered to spy on Chelsea's future cup opponents. The one team he failed to watch, Burnley, came closest to knocking the Blues out of the competition in the fourth round.
- Midfielder John Hollins was the only player allowed to pin up the opposition team sheet on the Chelsea dressing-room notice board.
- Defender Paddy Mulligan didn't play a single minute in the cup run, but was always listed on the official team-sheet beneath the 11 players and one permitted substitute. Mulligan was deemed to be 'lucky' because he had never appeared on a losing Chelsea side since signing from Shamrock Rovers in October 1969.
- Director Richard Attenborough was another lucky mascot. Appointed to the Chelsea board in November 1969, he didn't see the Blues lose once in the remainder of the season (the few league defeats the team suffered, including one at home in January 1970 to final opponents Leeds, occurred while 'Dickie' was out of the country on film business).
- Left-winger Peter Houseman always turned up in his club blazer on matchdays, even though the rule was that they only had to be worn on away trips.
- Dave Sexton refused to appear in team photographs until after the semi-final victory over Watford.
- Chairman Brian Mears only wore his gold tie pin on FA Cup days.
- At the start of the cup run four Chelsea players, Charlie Cooke, Ian Hutchinson, Alan Hudson and David Webb, vowed not to have a haircut until the Blues were knocked out or won the trophy. As each

round passed, more players joined them in boycotting the barbers' with the result that Chelsea were the hairiest ever team to lift the cup.

— PREMIERSHIP CHAMPIONS 2006 —

Chelsea won back-to-back league titles for the first time in season 2005/06, confirming their triumph with an emphatic 3–0 victory over Manchester United at Stamford Bridge. The Blues' home form was sensational throughout the campaign, with only Charlton managing to leave SW6 undefeated. At the end of the season the top of the Premiership table looked like this:

	P	W	D	L	F	A	W	D	L	F	A	Pts
Chelsea	38	18	1	0	47	9	11	3	5	25	13	91
Man Utd	38	13	5	1	37	8	12	3	4	35	26	83
Liverpool	38	15	3	1	32	8	10	4	5	25	17	82

— NEW DOUBLE —

Chelsea became only the third English club to win the so-called 'New Double' of league championship and League Cup (after Nottingham Forest in 1978 and Liverpool in 1982–84). Manchester United have since won the same double in 2009.

— STALWARTS REWARDED —

Chelsea have given many long-serving players well-deserved testimonials. Here is a selection of results from those matches:

Player	Year	Result
Ken Shellito	1968	Chelsea 6 QPR 3
Peter Bonetti	1971	Chelsea 1 Standard Liege 2
Peter Houseman	1973	Chelsea 4 Fulham 1
Eddie McCreadie	1974	Chelsea 1 Manchester United 2
John Hollins	1974	Chelsea 1 Arsenal 1
Peter Osgood	1975	Chelsea 4 Chelsea Past XI 3
Marvin Hinton	1976	Chelsea 2 Crystal Palace 2
Ian Hutchinson	1978	Chelsea 2 QPR 2
Charlie Cooke	1978	Chelsea 2 Crystal Palace 0
Peter Bonetti	1979	Chelsea 5 Manchester United 3
John Dempsey	1980	Chelsea 5 International XI 3
Ron Harris	1980	Chelsea 0 Chelsea Past XI 1
Mickey Droy	1983	Chelsea 2 Arsenal 1
John Bumstead	1987	Chelsea 1 Real Sociedad 0

Colin Pates	1988	Chelsea 0 Tottenham 0
Eddie Niedzwiecki	1989	Chelsea 5 Chelsea 1984/85 4
Kerry Dixon	1995	Chelsea 5 Tottenham 1
Paul Elliott	1995	Chelsea 1 Porto 1
Steve Clarke	1996	Chelsea 2 PSV 3
Kevin Hitchcock	1998	Chelsea 3 Nottingham Forest 3
Dennis Wise	1999	Chelsea 0 Bologna 0
Gianfranco Zola	2004	Chelsea 3 Real Zaragoza 0*

* Tribute match

— THE GOD SQUAD —

The Chelsea players who sought inspiration from above:

- **Nicolas Anelka:** In 2004 Anelka converted to Islam, adopting the Muslim name Abdul-Salam Bilal. "The subject fascinates me, just like astronomy does," he said at the time. His faith was a factor in his move to Turkish side Fenerbahce in 2005, although he only stayed a year before returning to England with Bolton. Anelka's decision to sign for Chelsea in January 2008 attracted criticism from some hard-line Muslims, who were opposed to him playing for a 'Jewish club'.
- **Peter Bonetti:** A practicing Roman Catholic, Bonetti would regularly attend mass in a local church when Chelsea were on tour, often accompanied by his manager, Dave Sexton.
- **Glenn Hoddle:** The Chelsea player-manager found God in the mid-80s while at Tottenham, leading comedian Jasper Carrott to quip "That must have been one hell of a pass." Hoddle's belief in reincarnation – specifically the notion that disabled people are being punished for sins committed in a previous life – famously led to his dismissal as England manager in 1999.
- **Mateja Kezman:** An Orthodox Christian, the Serb striker has a number of tattoos with religious themes. "Religion is very important to me," Kezman once said. "It is the central thing in my life. When I wear a T-shirt with Jesus on, it is not just a fashion statement, it is because it really means something to me."
- **Gavin Peacock:** Briefly Chelsea captain under fellow believer Glenn Hoddle, Peacock became a Christian in his late teens. "There were no flashing lights or dramatic conversion story to tell," he told the Salvation Army newspaper *War Cry*, "but a growing, gradual solid realisation of God's presence in my life." In February 2008 Peacock, who is now studying for a theology degree in Canada, fulfilled a long-term ambition when he presented the BBC programme *Songs of Praise*.
- **Bobby Tambling:** Chelsea's all-time leading goalscorer has suggested

that becoming a Jehovah's Witness might have led to the Blues selling him to Crystal Palace in the summer of 1970. "Peter Knowles had become a Witness at Wolves and had packed up football," he said, "and perhaps Chelsea thought, 'God, this fellow could turn round one day and tell us he's not going to play anymore, we'd better see if we can get some money for him.'"

• **George Weah:** Formerly a Muslim, Weah converted to Christianity a few years before joining Chelsea on loan from AC Milan in January 2000. "I pray for peace for everybody," he once said, "for Muslim and Christian, for black, white, green, yellow and brown." Nice of him to include the green people, who don't always get a mention . . .

— ROMAN'S MANAGERS —

Since he bought Chelsea in 2003, Roman Abramovich hasn't exactly been shy of making changes in the Blues' dug-out: to date, he has employed six managers and two caretakers in his nine years at the Bridge. Remarkably, given the fact that some of the bosses only lasted a matter of months, all of his appointments enjoyed pretty decent records – as this table illustrates:

Manager	P	W	D	L	F	A	Win %
Claudio Ranieri (2003–04)	59	36	12	11	102	48	61.02
Jose Mourinho (2004–08)	185	124	40	21	330	119	67.03
Avram Grant (2007–08)	54	36	13	5	97	36	66.67
Luiz Felipe Scolari (2008–09)	36	20	11	5	66	22	55.56
Ray Wilkins (2009)*	1	1	0	0	3	1	100
Guus Hiddink (2009)*	22	16	5	1	41	19	72.73
Carlo Ancelotti (2009–11)	109	67	20	22	241	93	61.47
Andre Villas Boas (2011–12)	40	19	11	10	69	43	47.50
Roberto di Matteo (2012–)	21	13	5	3	43	23	61.90

* Caretaker manager

The stats reveal that:

• Discounting the one match for which Ray Wilkins was in charge, caretaker boss Guus Hiddink enjoyed the best record of all of Abramovich's managers, leading the Blues to victory in 16 out of 22 games – a win rate of 72.73%. Jose Mourinho, Chelsea's most successful manager ever in terms of silverware, enjoyed a win rate of 67.03%, putting him second on the list.

• The Blues were most prolific in front of goal during the reign of Italian boss Carlo Ancelotti, scoring an average of 2.21 goals per game.

- Surprisingly, perhaps, Chelsea's defence was at its meanest during the short-lived tenure of Brazilian boss Luiz Felipe Scolari, the Blues conceding an average of just 0.61 goals per game.
- The least successful Chelsea manager of the Abramovich era by some distance was Andre Villas Boas, the Blues winning just under half of the 40 games for which he was in charge.

— THAT'S MY BALL! —

On 14 May 1977 Chelsea celebrated promotion back to the First Division by thrashing Hull City 4–0 at Stamford Bridge in front of 43,718 ecstatic fans. Star of the show was striker Steve Finnieston, who scored the first hat-trick of his career. As the match neared its conclusion, Finnieston's thoughts turned to the match ball. He desperately wanted to keep the ball as a memento but, with hundreds of jubilant young Chelsea fans preparing to invade the pitch, he also knew that getting hold of the prize would not be easy:

> "The ref said, 'Get ready to run off, because I'm going to blow the final whistle.' So everyone ran off except me because I wanted the ball. I managed to get it from Peter Bonetti's goal kick, but I was on the centre spot and got completely mobbed. I really thought I was going to die from lack of oxygen. It was quite frightening. Everybody was pulling at my kit. I lost my boots, shorts and socks, but I managed to keep hold of my shirt, although it got ripped, and the ball."

Back in the safety of the dressing-room, Finnieston got his teammates to sign the ball for him. He still has the ball today and it remains one of his most cherished reminders of his career in the game.

— THE BLUES' GREATEST MOMENTS . . . EVER! —

In 2005, the club's centenary year, Chelsea TV invited fans to vote for their three favourite moments in the Blues' history. When all the votes were counted up this was the Top 20:

1. Frank Lampard's goals at Bolton secure the Premiership title, 2005
2. Wayne Bridge's late winner knocks Arsenal out of the Champions League, 2004
3. Roberto di Matteo's 43-second opener sets up FA Cup glory, 1997
4. Roman Abramovich buys Chelsea, 2003
5. David Webb wins first FA Cup for the Blues, 1970
6. Gianfranco Zola nets with a backheel volley against Norwich, 2002
7. Blues fight back from 2–0 down to beat Liverpool in the FA Cup, 1997

8. Zola scores the winner in European Cup Winners' Cup Final, 1998
9. Peter Osgood's diving header in the FA Cup Final replay, 1970
10. Chelsea FC are formed, 1905
11. Chelsea beat Barcelona 4–2 in one of the all-time great games, 2005
12. The Blues lift FA Cup at the old Wembley for the last time, 2000
13. The Blues beat Liverpool to gain Champions League qualification, 2003
14. Ruud Gullit signs for Chelsea to begin an era of foreign stars at the Bridge, 1995
15. Clive Walker's winner saves the Blues from the drop to Division Three, 1983
16. The Blues stuff Lazio 4–0 in Rome, 2003
17. Treble winners Manchester United are humbled 5–0 at the Bridge, 1999
18. The Bridge is saved from the grasping hands of property developers, 1992
19. A first league win at Highbury for 15 years, 2005
20. Zola hits a cup semi special against Wimbledon, 1997

— MISCELLANEOUS SEASONAL RECORDS —

Highest points total: 99, 1988/89
Most league wins: 29, 1988/89, 2004/05 and 2005/06
Most home wins: 18, 1906/07 and 2005/06
Most away wins: 15, 2004/05
Fewest defeats: 1, 2004/05
Fewest home defeats: 0, 1910/11, 1976/77, 2004/05, 2005/06, 2006/07 and 2007/08
Fewest away defeats: 1, 2004/05

Lowest points total: 20, 1978/79
Fewest league wins: 5, 1978/79
Fewest home wins: 3, 1978/79
Fewest away wins: 0, 1914/15
Most defeats: 27, 1978/79
Most home defeats: 13, 1978/79
Most away defeats: 16, 1961/62

Most goals scored: 103, 2009/10
Most goals scored at home: 68, 2009/10
Most goals scored away: 46, 1988/89
Fewest goals conceded: 15, 2004/05
Fewest goals conceded at home: 6, 2004/05

Fewest goals conceded away: 9, 2004/05

Fewest goals scored: 31, 1923/24
Fewest goals scored at home: 17, 1921/22
Fewest goals scored away: 8, 1923/24
Most goals conceded: 100, 1960/61
Most goals conceded at home: 50, 1959/60
Most goals conceded away: 65, 1961/62

Most draws: 18, 1922/23
Most home draws: 13, 1922/23
Most away draws: 9, on eight occasions
Fewest draws: 3, 1997/98
Fewest home draws: 0, 1906/07
Fewest away draws: 1, 1962/63 and 1997/98

— HANDBAGS AT TEN PACES —

Football's a passionate game so it's not surprising that, over the years, Chelsea players and staff have been involved in a number of violent incidents on the pitch. Here are some of the most memorable clashes:

- Ted Drake and Stan Cullis (Wolves): The two bosses came to blows after Chelsea's dramatic 4–3 win at Molineux in December 1954. "Ted approached Cullis ready to shake his hand," recalled Blues skipper Roy Bentley. "Stan, stubborn as ever, refused and muttered something under his breath. Ted replied with his fists and landed a punch that knocked Stan over."
- Eddie McCreadie and Francesco Carpenetti (Roma): In a tempestuous Fairs Cup clash at the Bridge in October 1965 left-back McCreadie was sent off in the first half for throwing a punch at an opponent. "I went on an overlap, got my cross in, and this guy came across and kicked me in the shins," remembered Eddie. "Then he put his hand right round my throat. And I was, well, have some of that, you know. And I decked him." Despite being reduced to ten men, Chelsea still won the game 4–1.
- Mickey Thomas and Andy Blair (Sheffield Wednesday): In only his second game for the Blues following his transfer from Stoke in January 1984, Thomas reacted to taunts from the Wednesday midfielder about the end of his turbulent marriage to a former Miss Wales runner up. "He was dishing out loads of stick during the game so in the end I cracked and knocked him clean out with one punch," recalled Thomas. "The ref and linesmen didn't see it but the Chelsea fans

were cheering and singing, 'There's only one Mickey Thomas'."

- Nigel Spackman and Martin Keown (Arsenal): The normally mild-mannered Spackers was sent off after whacking the Arsenal defender towards the end of the Blues 1–0 win at the Bridge in September 1995. "Martin Keown tried to elbow me and missed, and I just lost it and punched him," he said later. "That was very unlike me. But I'd had a bad week as my little lad Frazer had just been diagnosed with cerebral palsy. I got a three-match ban for violent conduct. It was embarrassing, but I got the best standing ovation I've ever had as I left the pitch."

- Chelsea and Wimbledon: After a bad-tempered London derby at the Bridge in February 2000 at least 16 players became involved in a mass punch up in the tunnel as they headed towards their changing rooms. During the fracas, Wimbledon boss Egil Olsen was knocked to the floor and the fighting was only halted when police intervened. Chelsea attempted to downplay the incident, although assistant manager Gwyn Williams admitted, "Someone fell down the stairs and there was a scuffle." Both clubs were charged with misconduct by the FA and Chelsea were later fined £50,000 for their part in the affair. Blues skipper Dennis Wise, whose on-pitch clash with Wimbledon's Kenny Cunningham sparked the tunnel war, was also fined £7,500.

- Chelsea and Arsenal: The two sides were charged with misconduct after an injury-time brawl during the Blues' Carling Cup victory. The confrontation was sparked when Chelsea midfielder John Obi Mikel grabbed Kolo Toure's shirt and the Arsenal player reacted angrily. As the incident threatened to spiral out of control, Blues boss Jose Mourinho and Gunners manager Arsene Wenger rushed onto the pitch to act as peacemakers. After order was restored, referee Howard Webb sent off Mikel, Toure and another Arsenal player, Emanuel Adebayor, while Blues stand-in skipper Frank Lampard and Arsenal midfielder Cesc Fabregas were booked.

— CUP HOLDERS KO'D —

Chelsea have knocked out the reigning cup holders in the following competitions:

FA Cup

Year	Round	Result
1931	4th	Chelsea 2 Arsenal 1
1965	4th	West Ham 0 Chelsea 1
1966	3rd	Liverpool 1 Chelsea 2

League Cup

Year	Round	Result
1965	Final	Chelsea 3 Leicester City 2 (aggregate)
1971/72	Semi-final	Chelsea 5 Tottenham 4 (aggregate)

Champions League

Year	Round	Result
2012	Semi-final	Chelsea 3 Barcelona 2 (aggregate)

European Cup Winners' Cup

Year	Round	Result
1971	Semi-final	Chelsea 2 Manchester City 0 (aggregate)

— YOU DON'T KNOW WHAT YOU'RE DOING . . . —

The team selections that had Chelsea fans scratching their heads:

- After four consecutive defeats Chelsea manager Dave Sexton dropped Shed heroes Peter Osgood, Alan Hudson, Peter Bonetti and Tommy Baldwin from the Blues side for a match at Sheffield United on New Year's Day 1974. Following a furious row with Sexton, both Osgood and Hudson were placed on the transfer list and soon left the club. Chelsea did manage to win at Bramall Lane without the star quartet, but finished the season just one point clear of the relegation zone.

- Newly installed Blues boss Eddie McCreadie dropped seasoned pros John Hollins, Marvin Hinton, Peter Houseman and Steve Kember for a vital relegation match against fellow strugglers Tottenham at White Hart Lane in April 1975. In their place McCreadie picked youngsters Ian Britton, Teddy Maybank, John Sparrow and Ray Wilkins, appointing the 18-year-old Wilkins as captain. The gamble failed to pay off as Chelsea lost 2–0 and were relegated to the old Second Division a week later.

- In the autumn of 1986 John Hollins incurred the wrath of the Stamford Bridge faithful when he left out popular striker David Speedie and hard-running midfielder Nigel Spackman for a series of matches. As defeat followed defeat, the chants of 'Hollins out!' grew louder until the pair were eventually restored to the team for the Full Members Cup victory at West Ham in November 1986. Both players, though, were soon on the move – Spackman to Liverpool and Speedie to Coventry City.

- Claudio Ranieri lived up to his 'Tinkerman' nickname on more than one occasion, but never with more disastrous consequences than in the Champions League semi-final first leg against Monaco in April 2004. With the scores level at 1–1 at half-time, Ranieri bizarrely chose to replace Jesper Gronkjaer with a clearly unfit Juan Sebastian Veron. The Italian then made a serious of strange tactical decisions in the second half, including playing striker Jimmy Floyd Hasselbaink on the right wing and midfielder Scott Parker at right back, which contributed to Chelsea's eventual 3–1 defeat.

- Blues boss Avram Grant left England winger Joe Cole on the bench for the Carling Cup Final against Tottenham in February 2008, preferring instead to pair Didier Drogba in attack with new signing Nicolas Anelka for the first time. The plan backfired as Spurs won the match 2–1, with Anelka looking completely lost on the left wing.

- Embattled Chelsea manager Andre Villas-Boas had Blues fans scratching their heads when he left senior pros Ashley Cole, Frank Lampard and Michael Essien on the bench for the first leg of the Champions League last 16 tie away to Napoli. His team selection proved disastrous as the Blues crashed to a 3–1 defeat and, less than two weeks later, Villas-Boas was sacked.

— IT'S A GAME OF 90 MINUTES . . . EXCEPT FOR SWP —

Shaun-Wright Phillips didn't have the best of starts to his Chelsea career after signing from Manchester City for £21m in the summer of 2005. In his first season at the Bridge the diminutive winger failed to complete a Premiership match, being substituted in all of his ten starts and coming off the bench a further 17 times. It was a similar story in his second season, too, when he was again subbed off by Blues boss Jose Mourinho in his first four Premiership starts and featured off the bench a further 14 times. Finally, in his 46th Premiership match for Chelsea, at home to Sheffield United on 17 March 2007, SWP managed to play all 90 minutes of the game.

— STEIN'S PURPLE PATCH —

In the 1993/94 season Chelsea striker Mark Stein set a Premiership record by scoring in seven consecutive league matches. His goalscoring run began on 27 December 1993 with a consolation strike in a 3–1 defeat at Southampton and continued until 5 February 1994 when Stein scored twice in a 4–2 defeat at Everton. In between, the South African born striker also found the net against Newcastle, Swindon, Everton (2), Norwich and Aston Villa.

Stein's record was eventually beaten by Manchester United's Ruud van Nistelrooy, who scored in eight consecutive Premiership matches in the 2001/02 season.

— THE LONG AND THE SHORT OF IT —

Lanky Dutch goalkeeper Ed de Goey is the tallest player in Chelsea history. Standing at 6ft 6in, Ed is just one inch taller than the Blues' current No 1, Petr Cech.

The shortest player to appear for the Blues is Jackie Crawford. The 1920s inside forward was a mere 5ft 3in tall.

— KERRY'S AN EGGHEAD —

A list of Chelsea players who have made slightly surprising TV appearances:

Peter Bonetti: contestant, *The Weakest Link* (BBC1, 2002)

Kerry Dixon: team member, *Celebrity Eggheads* (BBC2, 2011)

Didier Drogba: guest, *The Graham Norton Show* (BBC1, 2012)

Frank Leboeuf: team member, *They Think It's All Over* (BBC1, 1998)

Graeme Le Saux: team member, *They Think It's All Over* (BBC1, 1997 and 2003); contestant, *The Weakest Link* (BBC1, 2005)

Roberto di Matteo: contestant, *Superstars* (Channel 5, 2008)

Gavin Peacock: presenter, *Songs of Praise* (BBC1, 2008)

Terry Venables: contestant, *All Star Mr & Mrs* (ITV, 2008); contestant, *Stars In Their Eyes* (ITV, 2000); guest, *Room 101* (BBC1, 2000)

— FIRST FOREIGN OPPONENTS —

Chelsea's first non-English opponents were Sparta Rotterdam, who played a friendly at Stamford Bridge on 17 April 1906. The Dutch side, who at the time were a powerful force in their domestic league, won the match 2–0.

— CHRISTMAS WISH COMES TRUE —

In December 1992 the Chelsea matchday programme asked a cross-section of supporters which player they would buy for the club, if money was no object. Among the big names on the fans' wish list were Alan Shearer, Paul Gascoigne, Eric Cantona, Marco van Basten, Roberto Baggio and, rather less excitingly, QPR winger Andy Sinton. Lee Boundy from Isleworth, though, aimed his sights highest of all: "I'd sign Ruud Gullit," he enthused. "He is a world class player and a fantastic striker."

In 1992 the prospect of a player of Gullit's stature signing for the Blues, who were then a mediocre Premiership side, seemed extremely remote. Yet, two and a half years later, the legendary Dutch international and former World Footballer of the Year pitched up at Stamford Bridge on a free transfer from Italian club Sampdoria. It may have seemed no more than a pipedream at the time, but Lee's Christmas wish had come true.

— HEY, HEY, WE'RE THE MONKEYS —

In the late 1990s Bristol Zoo named four black howler monkeys after Chelsea players. The baby monkey monikers – Zola (born 1997), Desailly (1998), Babayaro (1999) and Vialli (2000) – were chosen by primate overseer John Buchan, a committed fan of the Blues.

— DROGBA'S FINAL SCORING RECORDS —

- With four goals apiece in the Carling and FA Cup finals and one in the Champions League final, Didier Drogba is easily Chelsea's top scorer in major cup finals. His total of nine goals puts him well ahead of Peter Osgood (four goals in finals) and Roberto di Matteo (three goals). For good measure, Drogba also scored Chelsea's winning penalty in the shoot-out against Bayern Munich in the 2012 Champions League final.

- Drogba's total of four goals in the Carling Cup Final (one in 2005, two in 2007 and one in 2008) is a record for the competition. The only other player to have scored more than two goals in the final is Liverpool's Ronnie Whelan, who found the net three times when the Reds won the trophy four times on the trot between 1981 and 1984.

- In 2012 Drogba became the first player ever to score in four FA Cup finals, when he netted the Blues' second goal in their 2–1 win over Liverpool at Wembley. The Ivorian striker had previously got on the scoresheet in Chelsea's triumphs in 2007, 2009 and 2010 against Manchester United, Everton and Portsmouth respectively.

—LOAN STARS —

A team of Chelsea players who were sent out on loan to other clubs during their Stamford Bridge careers:

1. Dave Beasant (Grimsby, Wolves)
2. Glen Johnson (Portsmouth)
3. Wayne Bridge (Fulham)
4. David Lee (Reading, Plymouth, Portsmouth, Sheffield United)
5. John Terry (Nottingham Forest)
6. Michael Duberry (Bournemouth)
7. Scott Sinclair (Plymouth, QPR, Charlton, Crystal Palace)
8. Alexy Smertin (Portsmouth, Charlton)

9. Hernan Crespo (AC Milan)
10. Carlton Cole (Wolves, Charlton, Aston Villa)
11. Mikael Forssell (Crystal Palace, Borussia Monchengladbach, Birmingham City)

— GIVE US A SONG! —

According to Chelsea tradition, new arrivals at the club have to sing a song in front of the rest of the squad. Here's a selection of the ditties chosen by some of the current team:

Gary Cahill: *Sexy and I Know It*
Ashley Cole: *I'll Stand By You*
Frank Lampard: *Maybe It's Because I'm A Londoner*
John Terry: *My Old Man's A Dustman*
Fernando Torres: *You'll Never Walk Alone*
Ross Turnbull: *Wonderwall*

— CHELSEA'S ALL-TIME LEAGUE RECORD AGAINST 2012/13 PREMIERSHIP CLUBS —

| | | Home | | | | | Away | | | | |
	P	W	D	L	F	A	W	D	L	F	A
Arsenal	150	25	25	27	93	99	19	20	36	97	117
Everton	146	36	25	12	134	69	15	22	23	91	151
Man Utd	140	22	19	29	102	118	18	23	29	72	112
Liverpool	138	37	14	18	119	69	9	14	46	68	146
Man City	134	34	20	13	115	72	21	16	30	78	96
Newcastle	134	37	19	11	127	72	16	17	34	71	99
Aston Villa	130	33	13	19	104	80	15	19	31	87	119
Tottenham	128	31	14	19	91	76	22	8	24	95	106
West Brom	112	28	14	14	115	73	21	13	22	70	93
Sunderland	110	36	11	8	120	55	18	9	29	71	105
West Ham	86	22	9	12	80	61	13	8	22	59	77
Southampton	76	18	10	10	63	44	15	11	12	53	54
Stoke City	76	21	10	7	70	46	15	8	15	42	53
Fulham	66	19	12	2	53	25	19	9	5	58	35
QPR	42	11	6	4	34	24	4	9	8	24	31
Norwich	34	8	5	4	29	18	3	6	8	15	26
Swansea	20	6	3	1	27	9	2	4	4	7	13
Wigan	14	6	1	0	19	3	5	1	1	15	6
Reading	12	3	3	0	6	3	3	1	2	10	10

— WE LOVE YOU CHELSEA —

"Chelsea has always been my first love. I'd have liked to have spent the whole of my career at Stamford Bridge, but it was not to be. I always have a special place in my football heart for Chelsea."

1960s captain Terry Venables

"Becoming a Chelsea director was one of the most marvellous things that has happened in my life." **Lord Attenborough**

"The blue and the blue, with white socks – it was smart. It wasn't just Chelsea, it was smart." **1970s defender David Webb**

"Chelsea FC will never lose its identity. Chelsea will be Chelsea for always – and at Stamford Bridge." **Chelsea chairman Brian Mears, April 1977**

"I walk in here every day and you look out there and you get a tingling down your back. It's a tremendous set-up. Tremendous supporters."

John Neal, on his appointment as manager in 1981

"Managing Chelsea Football Club is without doubt the proudest moment in my football career so far."

Glenn Hoddle, in his last programme notes before becoming England manager, May 1996

"To wear the colours of Chelsea must be an honour."

Ruud Gullit in August 1996, shortly after his appointment as player/manager

"You Chelsea supporters have been unbelievable to me so far. I can't ask you for anything more now that I am player/manager."

Gianluca Vialli, after taking over as manager, February 1998

"Hello, Chelsea supporters. You may not have heard of me before I came to you last month, but I had heard of you. I knew that Chelsea are a good team in Europe and that the fans are great."

Claudio Ranieri, in his first programme notes, October 2000

"It feels good because it's a change, it's a big challenge, and I'm playing with players like Zola who I've been a massive fan of for years. To mix with players like that and train with them is brilliant."

Frank Lampard, shortly after joining Chelsea, July 2001

"You don't get many one-club players nowadays, but I definitely want to stay at Chelsea for the rest of my career."   **John Terry, November 2001**

"I played for Napoli and it was blue. I play for Chelsea and it's blue. Italy is blue. Blue belongs to me, my life."   **Gianfranco Zola, January 2002**

"As soon as I arrived here I instantly had a great feeling, it filled me with confidence, and it was clear to me I had to decide to come to Chelsea."   **Arjen Robben, December 2004**

"I'll be Blue, for sure."
Jose Mourinho gives his support to Chelsea before the 2012 Champions League Final

"At some clubs you just play for them and then once you're gone that's it, but the new regime at Chelsea has remembered that there were 99 years of history before they arrived."   **Pat Nevin, January 2006**

"If I'm still here, I hope I can be just like the old boys of '55 who came out and celebrated with us last season. They came with a lot of dignity, enjoyed their football, and I hope that will be me. I think I'll still be living in the area and watching Chelsea."
Frank Lampard looks forward 50 years, December 2005

"The first year was fantastic. The second year was not so good. I am not bitter or angry. Absolutely not. I consider Chelsea a really fantastic club."
Carlo Ancelotti looks back fondly on his two-year stay at the Bridge, August 2011

"We all have the same aim, to keep the Blue flag flying high."
Chelsea legend Didier Drogba, 2010

— CLUB V COUNTRY —

Chelsea have played a number of high-profile friendlies against national sides, most notably two games against West Germany in the build up to the 1966 World Cup. The Blues won the first encounter, in Duisberg in February 1965, by a single Barry Bridges goal, prompting German manager Helmet Schoen to say, "Considering their average age is under 22, Chelsea are a marvellous team. They are the best English club side I have seen for a long time."

A few months later, in August 1965, the teams met again in Essen, but this time the Germans restored some national pride with a narrow 3–2 win.

— FA CUP TOP MARKSMEN —

The following four Chelsea players have topped the scoring charts in the FA Cup in the Premier League era:

1994	Gavin Peacock	6 goals
2000	Gus Poyet	6 goals
2007	Frank Lampard	6 goals
2009	Nicolas Anelka*	4 goals

* Joint top scorer

— CHELSEA'S LEAGUE RECORD 1905–2012 —

	Div	P	W	D	L	F	A	W	D	L	F	A	Pts	Pos
1905/06	2	38	13	4	2	58	16	9	5	5	32	21	53	3rd
1906/07	2	38	18	0	1	55	10	8	5	6	25	24	57	2nd
														(Promoted)
1907/08	1	38	8	3	8	30	35	6	5	8	23	27	36	13th
1908/09	1	38	8	7	4	33	22	6	2	11	23	39	37	11th
1909/10	1	38	10	4	5	32	24	1	3	15	15	46	29	19th
														(Relegated)
1910/11	2	38	17	2	0	48	7	3	7	9	23	28	49	3rd
1911/12	2	38	15	2	2	36	13	9	4	6	26	21	54	2nd
														(Promoted)
1912/13	1	38	7	2	10	29	40	4	4	11	22	33	28	18th
1913/14	1	38	12	3	4	28	18	4	4	11	18	37	39	8th
1914/15	1	38	8	6	5	32	25	0	7	12	19	40	29	19th
1915/19							FIRST WORLD WAR							
1919/20	1	42	15	3	3	33	10	7	2	12	23	41	49	3rd
1920/21	1	42	9	7	5	35	24	4	6	11	13	34	39	18th
1921/22	1	42	9	6	6	17	16	8	6	7	23	27	46	9th
1922/23	1	42	5	13	3	29	20	4	5	12	16	33	36	19th
1923/24	1	42	7	9	5	23	21	2	5	14	8	32	32	21st
														(Relegated)
1924/25	2	42	11	8	2	31	12	5	7	9	20	35	47	5th
1925/26	2	42	10	7	4	42	22	9	7	5	34	27	52	3rd
1926/27	2	42	13	7	1	40	17	7	5	9	22	35	52	4th
1927/28	2	42	15	2	4	46	15	8	6	7	29	30	54	3rd
1928/29	2	42	10	6	5	40	30	7	4	10	24	35	44	9th
1929/30	2	42	17	3	1	49	14	5	8	8	25	32	55	2nd
														(Promoted)
1930/31	1	42	13	4	4	42	19	2	6	13	22	48	40	12th
1931/32	1	42	12	4	5	43	27	4	4	13	26	46	40	12th
1932/33	1	42	9	4	8	38	29	5	3	13	25	44	35	18th
1933/34	1	42	12	3	6	44	24	2	5	14	23	45	36	19th
1934/35	1	42	11	5	5	49	32	5	4	12	24	50	41	12th
1935/36	1	42	11	7	3	39	27	4	6	11	26	45	43	8th
1936/37	1	42	11	6	4	36	21	3	7	11	16	34	41	13th
1937/38	1	42	11	6	4	40	22	3	7	11	25	43	41	10th
1938/39	1	42	10	5	6	43	29	2	4	15	21	51	33	20th
1939/46							SECOND WORLD WAR							
1946/47	1	42	9	3	9	33	39	7	4	10	36	45	39	15th

1947/48	1	42	11	6	4	38	27	3	3	15	15	44	37	18th
1948/49	1	42	10	6	5	43	27	2	8	11	26	41	38	13th
1949/50	1	42	7	7	7	31	30	5	9	7	27	35	40	13th
1950/51	1	42	9	4	8	31	25	3	4	14	22	40	32	20th
1951/52	1	42	10	3	8	31	29	4	5	12	21	43	36	19th
1952/53	1	42	10	4	7	35	24	2	7	12	21	42	35	19th
1953/54	1	42	12	3	6	45	26	4	9	8	29	42	44	8th
1954/55	1	42	11	5	5	43	29	9	7	5	38	28	52	1st (Champions)
1955/56	1	42	10	4	7	32	26	4	7	10	32	51	39	16th
1956/57	1	42	7	8	6	43	36	6	5	10	30	37	39	13th
1957/58	1	42	10	5	6	47	34	5	7	9	36	45	42	11th
1958/59	1	42	13	2	6	52	37	5	2	14	25	61	40	14th
1959/60	1	42	7	5	9	44	50	7	4	10	32	41	37	18th
1960/61	1	42	10	5	6	61	48	5	2	14	37	52	37	12th
1961/62	1	42	7	7	7	34	29	2	3	16	29	65	28	22nd (Relegated)
1962/63	2	42	15	3	3	54	16	9	1	11	27	26	52	2nd (Promoted)
1963/64	1	42	12	3	6	36	24	8	7	6	36	32	50	5th
1964/65	1	42	15	2	4	48	19	9	6	6	41	35	56	3rd
1965/66	1	42	11	4	6	30	21	11	3	7	35	32	51	5th
1966/67	1	42	7	9	5	33	29	8	5	8	34	33	44	9th
1967/68	1	42	11	7	3	34	25	7	5	9	28	43	48	6th
1968/69	1	42	11	7	3	40	24	9	3	9	33	29	50	5th
1969/70	1	42	13	7	1	36	18	8	6	7	34	32	55	3rd
1970/71	1	42	12	6	3	34	21	6	9	6	18	21	51	6th
1971/72	1	42	12	7	2	41	20	6	5	10	17	29	48	7th
1972/73	1	42	9	6	6	30	22	4	8	9	19	29	40	12th
1973/74	1	42	9	4	8	36	29	3	9	9	20	31	37	17th
1974/75	1	42	4	9	8	22	31	5	6	10	20	41	33	21st (Relegated)
1975/76	2	42	7	9	5	25	20	5	7	9	28	34	40	11th
1976/77	2	42	15	6	0	51	22	6	7	8	22	31	55	2nd (Promoted)
1977/78	1	42	7	11	3	28	20	4	3	14	18	49	36	16th
1978/79	1	42	3	5	13	23	42	2	5	14	21	50	20	22nd (Relegated)
1979/80	2	42	14	3	4	34	16	9	4	8	32	36	53	4th